AND THAT'S THE WAY IT WAS...
GIVE OR TAKE

Also by Chris Gay

Shouldn't Ice Cold Beer Be Frozen?
My 365 Random Thoughts To Improve Your Life Not One Iota

AND THAT'S THE WAY IT WAS...
GIVE OR TAKE

A Daily Dose of My Radio Writings

by
Chris Gay

Suesea

And That's the Way It Was... Give or Take:
A Daily Dose of My Radio Writings

by Chris Gay

Published by
Suesea
P.O. 8063
Manchester, Connecticut 06040
www.suesea.com

First Edition

ISBN: 978-0-9844673-7-2

Book design and composition: www.dmargulis.com

"There are no fools so troublesome as those that have wit."

"If all printers were determined not to print anything till they were sure it would offend nobody, there would be very little printed."

"Either write things worth reading, or do things worth the writing."

—Ben Franklin

DEDICATION

This book is dedicated to all those who recognize
the necessity of humor in life. Laugh at yourselves
and each other; the truth is we're all in this together.

Also, to Bill
While genealogy brands you my uncle,
you'll always be a brother to me.

INTRODUCTION

Here we are once again, you and me. How've you been? I'm guessing we haven't spoken since you read the intro to my last book. So let me give you a quick overview of this book, because of its dissimilarity from its predecessor. (Yeah, I know a sentence like that last one doesn't really belong here, but occasionally I like to take my thesaurus out for a spin) I'll tell you a little about myself and why this book exists. I'm a freelance writer, broadcaster and voice-over artist. I do different types of writing and voice work—some comedy, some not. At times, my writing and voice work overlap, such as writing and voicing radio commercials. Over the past few years, I've further combined the two by writing and broadcasting a daily, sponsored, humor spot on the radio in the Hartford, Connecticut, market. This book is a collection of those daily historical humor broadcasts, combined with new material I've written to be broadcast in the near future. I've written jokes based on whatever humor-worthy historic events have occurred on each date of the calendar. So I guess you *could* say that this book is a few thousand years in the making. Please, though—don't say that. My humor leans toward dry and sarcastic; so politics makes for great source material. I'm also quite fond of the double entendre. Additionally, included here are numerous references to pop culture, music, sports, and everyday occurrences. (My guess is you know this already; as there's no way you didn't already open this book to a random page and check out some jokes before you bothered to read this introduction.) My goal as a humorist is to give you with something to think about—at least most of the time. Luckily, you have roughly 750 chances to help me accomplish that goal. Good luck, and all the best to you. Maybe someday I'll expand my radio spots outside New England and you can hear me for yourself. Today Hartford—tomorrow Buffalo. Or Omaha. A man can dream, can't he?

AND THAT'S THE WAY IT WAS...
GIVE OR TAKE

1935 College football's first Sugar and Orange Bowls were played. The following year they merged, and become the Tang Bowl.

⳹⳼

1928 The first U.S. office building to feature air-conditioning opened in San Antonio, Texas. Refusing to be outdone by the South, the North built the first office building enclosed entirely within a sauna, in Caribou, Maine.

1839 French photographer Louis Daguerre took the first photograph of the moon, though he was never able to fully comprehend the gravity of what he was looking at.

⳹⳼

1974 Richard Nixon imposed the 55 MPH speed limit. Subsequent studies showed the law was strictly obeyed, and only broken on those occasions when any person in America started up his or her car, then drove virtually anywhere.

1961 The U.S. severed our diplomatic relations with Cuba. So I guess you could say that we were close, but no more cigars.

⳹⳼

1888 Marvin Stone patented the wax drinking straw, which the public quickly chewed right up and spit right out.

1948 Britain granted Burma its independence. Evidently, they didn't want to bother waiting for Burma to just take it from them, like everyone else.

৪৩৫৪

1854 The McDonald Islands were discovered and finally, at long last, Grimace, the Hamburglar and Mayor McCheese were rescued and brought home to the delight of the adoring masses.

1781 Benedict Arnold completely destroyed Richmond, Virginia. When called out as a traitor by the vanquished townsfolk, Arnold responded that he preferred to call it free agency.

৪৩৫৪

1836 Davy Crockett arrived in Texas just in time for the battle of the Alamo. He was overheard by a local citizen muttering to himself that he really, really needed to work on his timing.

1845 Riots erupted in Stratford, Ontario. Eighty men fought in the streets for hours, until one of them suddenly realized there wasn't even a soccer match scheduled for that day.

৪৩৫৪

1942 Pan American Airlines became the first commercial airline to plan a flight around the world. It sounded good on paper, but was shelved once Pan Am realized that no one wanted to pay a colossal fare simply to end up right back where they started from.

☞ *Born on this date: Benjamin Franklin (1706—Old Style Calendar) American printer, Founding Father, statesman, inventor, revolutionary, doctor, humorist, and superlative user-upper.* ☜

1927 The first transatlantic telephone call took place between New York City and London, England. It was cut short however when both countries realized that they'd completely forgotten to consider the roaming charges.

୬୦୯ଓ

1994 Tonya Harding won the United States Female Figure Skating championship. However to be fair, she did have a leg up on Nancy Kerrigan.

1835 For the only time in United States history, our national debt was $0. Alarmed at the news, Congress immediately convened, then voted unanimously to charge a yacht to their Master Card in the hopes of preventing something so fiscally responsible from ever happening again.

୬୦୯ଓ

1642 Astronomer Galileo Galilei died in Arcetri, Italy. His last words lamented his only regret, that he'd never named a star after himself with the International Star Registry.

1788 Connecticut became the fifth state of the Union. Sales to the public of foam fingers bearing the slogan *We're #5!* didn't sell as well as the legislature had hoped, however.

୬୦୯ଓ

1986 After losing a patent battle to Polaroid, Kodak was obligated to stop making their instant cameras, thus giving Polaroid a victory in what may have, at this point, become the most irrelevant lawsuit in history.

1776   Thomas Paine published his pamphlet *Common Sense,* which was subsequently read and considered by our Founding Fathers of the Second Continental Congress and then, seemingly, by no succeeding Congress since.

ഇൽ൘

1945   No one was elected to the baseball Hall of Fame in Cooperstown, New York. At his induction ceremony, No One came off as somewhat cocky, constantly referring to himself in the third person, stating such things as, "No One had a good enough year to be enshrined, No One really distinguished himself, and No One really deserves to be here this year."

1878   For the first time, milk was delivered in glass bottles. This innovation made things much easier on consumers, who until then had spent hours daily trying to get the cows to stand directly over their cereal bowls.

ഇൽ൘

1949   For the first time in recorded history, snowfall occurred in Los Angeles, California. Evidently it came courtesy of Satan, as a result of the Clippers winning a playoff game.

1773   The first public museum in the United States was founded in Charleston, South Carolina. Its curator couldn't figure out why no patrons ever came in, until the janitor pointed out that the U.S. wouldn't be established for another three years.

1969   The New York Jets shocked the football world by defeating the Baltimore Colts 16–7 in Super Bowl III. This began a long and storied history of Jets success that includes winning Super Bowl III in 1969 and … winning Super Bowl III in 1969.

1989   At age 16 on a snowy Friday the 13th, I earned my Connecticut driver's license. The feeling of utter euphoria lasted precisely until the second I realized that, on its own, laminated cardboard got only zero miles to the gallon.

෨෮

1968   Johnny Cash recorded a live concert at California's Folsom Prison. Afterward he privately scolded his agent, telling him that that wasn't what he'd meant when he'd said he wanted to play a few bars.

1968   The Beatles completed their legendary *White Album.* With the music portion finished, they then took an extra 13 seconds to design the album's cover.

෨෮

1978   *Rescue From Gilligan's Island,* the first movie produced from a television series, premiered. It was a shrewd move indeed, as NBC wisely made sure that they didn't set the bar too high for future, similar productions.

1885   Wilson Bentley took the first photograph of a snowflake—or so he'd thought. It turned out to be just one of the Wonder Twins screwing with him.

1777 Citizens of New Connecticut, later the State of Vermont, declared their independence, though their legislature's minutes showed that it was primarily to ensure their spot as the 14th state quarter, when issued in 2001.

☞ *Born on this date: Dr. Martin Luther King, Jr. (1929)—American Civil Rights hero, and a man who proved that truly, character is King.* ☜

1962 Filming began on the first James Bond movie, Dr. No. The intense pressure of bringing Ian Fleming's iconic literary character to the big screen left the producers shaken, though not stirred.

&Cß

1974 Peter Benchley's novel *Jaws* was published, and then quickly reached the best seller list. It was described by one prominent '70s book reviewer as "a gripping story with a great deal of bite. There's no question that it reels you in hook, line and sinker."

1997 The National Basketball Association fined Dennis Rodman $25,000 for kicking a cameraman. So it could be said that, perhaps, a picture *is* worth a thousand words—and $25,000.

&Cß

1970 Willie Mays was named The Sporting News 1960s Player of the Decade. By all accounts however, the true 1960s "Player of the Decade," was Wilt Chamberlain.

☞ *Born on this date: Benjamin Franklin (1706—New Style Calendar) I wonder how he took the news that, out of the blue, he'd have to wait an extra 11 days to legally barhop.* ☜

1911   The first instance of an aircraft landing on a ship occurred in San Francisco harbor. It worked out much better than the original attempt, where it was tried the other way around.

ಬಂಞ

1981   Iran decided to accept the United States's offer of $7.9 billion in frozen assets. Just out of curiosity, how long—in seconds—do you think actually they took to mull it over?

1955   The board game Scrabble debuted. It was an immediate … an immediate … damn, what's the word I'm looking for?

ಬಂಞ

1915   George Claude patented the neon sign, then was promptly arrested for flashing.

1949   J. Edgar Hoover gave Shirley Temple a tear gas fountain pen, apparently in an attempt to prove that the pen was, indeed, mightier than the sword.

ಬಂಞ

1809   William MacLure published the first book on geology in the United States. One book reviewer wrote that he wasn't able to get through it as easily as he'd thought he would, stating he'd discovered it had some very rocky parts to it.

1986   On a 38° day in Indiana, a hundred people participated in the Nude Olympics race. At the finish line, a spectator commented to nearby reporters that it "Sure was one cold-ass day out."

৵৩

1677   In Boston, Massachusetts, a smallpox pamphlet became the first medical publication in America. Regarding the disease, it provided the best medical treatment of its time: sternly advising its readers to "not get it."

1506   The first contingent of 150 Swiss Guards arrived at the Vatican, carrying with them the cutest, most versatile little knives you ever saw.

৵৩

1947   The first commercial TV station west of the Mississippi River went on the air and finally, at long last, citizens on the left half of our country had access to the same crap that those of us on the right half did.

৵৩

1901   Queen Victoria passed away after 63 years on the British throne. You'd think that at some point she would have tried a different diet.

1985   Former Buffalo Bills running back O.J. Simpson became the first Heisman Trophy winner elected to the Football Hall of Fame. Simpson went on to have a brief acting career before ultimately fading out of the public spotlight, and into a life of relative obscurity.

৪০৫৪

1996 The first version of the Java programming language was released, with the only system bug being that all it knew how to do was ask for coffee.

1924 St. Petersburg, Russia, was officially renamed Leningrad, an action that immediately bankrupted the pre-existing local post card industry.

৪০৫৪

1952 Vincent Massey was sworn in as the first Canadian born Governor-General of Canada. You know it could just be me, but it doesn't seem like that sort of thing should've taken so long.

1890 The United Mine Workers of America was founded, under the slogan, What's Mined, Is Ours.

৪০৫৪

1918 Russia was declared a republic of Soviets. Well, duh.

৪০৫৪

1870 Gustavus Dows received a patent for the modern soda fountain. It was said that once behind that fountain, Dows turned into an incredible jerk. (*Author's Note: Hey, I wanted to do at least one joke for any centurions who may be reading this book.*)

1962 The space probe Ranger 3 was launched to the moon but missed it by 22,000 miles. Off by that much, my guess is that Johnny Damon tried to throw it there.

৪০০৪

1802   Congress passed an act calling for a library to be established within the U.S. Capitol, apparently so that members would have a place to go where no one would ever think to look for them.

৪০০৪

1930   The Terminal Tower opened in Cleveland, Ohio. I guess we should just be grateful its owner wasn't in charge of naming hospital wings.

☞   *Born on this date: Paul Newman (1925)—American actor/ philanthropist. Newman won an Oscar, starred in an ice hockey flick, and somehow found the time to improve my garden salad. Mere accolades don't do him justice.* 🖝

1967   More than sixty nations signed the Outer Space Treaty banning nuclear weapons in space. Per Section 1977, Paragraph IV of the treaty however, light sabers were still acceptable.

৪০০৪

1967   The New Orleans Saints signed the franchise's first player, then promptly asked him what number he wanted stitched into the side of his brown paper bag.

1495   Pope Alexander VI gave his son Cesare Borgia, whom he'd had with his mistress, as a hostage to France's King Charles VIII. Wait—hold on a second; the Pope gave his what, that he'd had with his who?

৪০০৪

1962 Johannes Relleke was stung 2,443 times by bees, which caused him to completely rethink his penchant for dressing up as a jar of honey at company picnics.

৪০০৪

1887 A snowstorm in Montana produced the world's largest recorded snowflakes at 15 inches wide by 8 inches thick. I'll take their word for it, but I could swear I've known bigger flakes than that.

1996 President Jacques Chirac announced a definitive end to French nuclear testing, which explains why Matthew Broderick never got to do the Godzilla sequel.

৪০০৪

1613 Galileo observed the planet Neptune, though failed to recognize it. On the one hand, maybe he deserves the chastising; on the other, perhaps he didn't identify it because it wasn't discovered for another 233 years.

1936 The new owners of the Boston Braves asked newspapermen to choose a new nickname for the team. Unfortunately for Massachusetts, the winning entry ultimately chosen turned out to be "Milwaukee."

৪০০৪

1661 England's Oliver Cromwell was ritually executed after having been dead for two years. That, my friends, is what's known as holding onto a grudge.

1847 Yerba Buena, California, was rechristened San Francisco. The act was due to an all out effort by the Chamber of Commerce to help Tony Bennett write a catchier song title.

31

1930 3M first marketed Scotch tape. It was very similar to other tape, in fact so much so that it could only be told apart by its distinctive brogue.

1948 The magnetic tape recorder was developed. The machine itself worked great; the problem was that they couldn't stop silverware from sticking to it.

FEBRUARY

1

1964 Indiana Governor Mathew Welsh attempted to ban the song *Louie, Louie* for its use of obscenities. Evidently, that also made Welsh the first person in America able to decipher its lyrics.

1920 The Royal Canadian Mounted Police was established. It was Canada's first truly concerted effort to capture Snidely Whiplash.

2

1993 Bill Murray woke up in Punxsutawney, Pennsylvania on Groundhog Day, and was made to repeat the same day over and over and over again in perpetuity.

છ૭ભ

1993   Bill Murray woke up in Punxsutawney, Pennsylvania on Groundhog Day, and was made to repeat the same day over and over and over again in perpetuity.

છ૭ભ

1993   Bill Murray woke up in Punxsutawney, Pennsylvania on Groundhog Day, and was made to repeat the same day over and over and over again in perpetuity.

1913   The 16th Amendment to the United States Constitution was ratified, authorizing the federal government to impose and collect an income tax. And thus, the term *Pandora's Box* was born.

છ૭ભ

1690   America's first paper money was issued by the Massachusetts Bay colony. The good news is that there's still some of that currency left today—primarily because in 1690 Wall Street hadn't been formed yet.

☞   *Born on this date: Norman Rockwell (1894) Legendary American painter/illustrator. His work has always inspired me. To write, not illustrate. I couldn't draw a straight line if you tied my hand to M.C. Escher's. I couldn't compose a stick figure with a ruler. All right—you get the picture (though still, I couldn't draw it).* 👉

1977   Fleetwood Mac released their eventual Grammy-winning album *Rumours*. Or at least that's what I've heard.

છ૭ભ

1789 George Washington was elected the first president of the United States of America. Washington brought to his new nation's highest office great character, honor and credibility, setting a precedent that at least four or five other presidents have followed since.

1825 Hannah Lord Montague of New York created the first detachable shirt collar. His original intent was to use it as a civilian crime stopping device, similar to Wonder Woman's golden tiara.

෨෬

1783 Sweden recognized the independence of the United States, though in secret they admitted that it was so they could get right to work building their first ten IKEA stores here.

1971 On the Apollo 14 Mission Alan Shepard became the first person to hit a golf ball on the Moon. This allowed millions of Americans who were tired of having to watch their tax dollars at work, finally get a chance to see them at play.

෨෬

1911 Rolls-Royce adopted the *Spirit of Ecstasy* mascot, which evidently just beat out the monocled, mustachioed, top hat sporting Rich Uncle Pennybags, who later went to work for Monopoly.

☞ *Born on this date: Ronald Reagan (1911)—40th U.S. president; guided America to victory in the Cold War. President Reagan also had careers as an actor and sportscaster. Though never a carpenter, he was still very proficient at tearing down walls.* ☜

1979   Pluto moved inside Neptune's orbit for the first time. Taking great exception to the encroachment, Neptune kicked its ass.

‍ॐ‍ও

1984   American astronaut Bruce McCandless made the first untethered space walk, sending a dejected Michael Jackson back to the drawing board.

1587   Mary Queen of Scots was beheaded, leaving many guys named Scot totally without leadership.

‍ॐ‍ও

1910   The Boy Scouts of America was incorporated. Then, in a decision that would haunt the organization for a century, they took a pass on the option to sell extraordinarily tasty, prepackaged cookies.

1986   In Egypt, British archaeologist Geoffrey Martin found the tomb of Maya, King Tut's treasurer. This may very well have been the most committed attempt in history to follow the money.

‍ॐ‍ও

1870   The U.S. Weather Bureau was established. In an unrelated story, 10 minutes later the first erroneous weather forecast was predicted.

1863   In a wedding orchestrated by P.T. Barnum, famed dwarfs General Tom Thumb and Lavinia Warren were married in New York City. By all accounts it was an exceptionally short ceremony.

৪০৫৪

1940   Hanna–Barbera's cartoon Tom and Jerry made its debut and, decades later, the two still play their silly game of cat and mouse.

1977   A 44 lb. lobster was caught off Nova Scotia then sold to a New York restaurant. It became an instant sensation and, though it didn't misbehave, regardless soon found itself in very hot water.

৪০৫৪

1960   Tonight Show host Jack Paar walked off of his own television show. Displaying such emotion was not out of the ordinary for him, with one colleague even commenting that the action was pretty much Paar for the course.

1879   The first artificial ice rink in North America opened at New York City's Madison Square Garden. It had been scheduled for completion in 1876, but scientists couldn't perfect the artificial water in time.

৪০৫৪

2000   Charles M. Schulz, creator of the beloved Charlie Brown comic strip, passed away. Quite admirably, he tirelessly worked his entire adult life for Peanuts.

☞ *Born on this date: Abraham Lincoln (1809)—first Republican president, 16th overall. Lincoln was the first pick in the 1860 presidential entry draft, ahead of Democrat Stephen Douglas and quarterback Ryan Leaf, who was then taken by the San Diego Chargers.* 👈

1837   An illegal riot occurred over the high price of flour in New York. Afterward, it took police almost a month to sift through the evidence.

છाজ

1689   William and Mary were proclaimed co-rulers of England, though the ruthless William was able to cunningly claim the better parking spot.

1971   Richard Nixon installed a secret taping system in the White House, obviously, in a shrewd attempt to protect himself from having the opportunity to later invoke his Fifth Amendment right.

છाজ

Today is St. Valentine's Day or, as both Hallmark and Russell Stover refer to it—Christmas.

1979   Australian Paul Shirley sucked a lifesaver for almost 4¾ hours. I'm guessing that this is one guy who had absolutely no idea how many licks it took to get to the center of a Tootsie Pop.

છाজ

1965   John Lennon passed his driving test at the age of 24. He then expressed relief that he'd no longer need to purchase a ticket to ride.

☞   *Born on this date: Susan B. Anthony (1820) Ms. Anthony was a pioneer in the movement toward women's rights and suffrage. She also spent time in Seneca Falls, New York, which has been theorized to be the inspiration for "Bedford Falls," Jimmy Stewart's fictional hometown in "It's A Wonderful Life." Hey, that was a great movie. I'm just saying.*

16

600   Pope Gregory the Great decreed that saying "God bless you" would be the correct response to a sneeze. He then added an exception for atheists, for whom he indicated the correct response was, "go to hell."

೮ഠന്മ

1968   In Haleyville, Alabama, the first 9-1-1 emergency telephone system went into service. My assumption is that they wanted to bring the system along slowly, with the population of Haleyville consistently less than the number of EMTs who manned the town's ambulance.

೮ഠന്മ

Bonus: 1918   Lithuania declared its independence. No joke here; I'm just honoring my great-grandmother. If you've ever wondered where I got my height, hair, and three-point range, well, now you know.

1996   World chess champion Garry Kasparov beat IBM super-computer *Deep Blue,* winning a six-game match in Philadelphia. Kasparov taunted Blue later at the post-match press conference, indicating that at least you can count on him when the chips are down.

જી03

1854   Great Britain recognized the independence of the Orange Free State. Judging by the price of juice, I can only assume they weren't talking about Florida.

1564   Michelangelo died in Rome. The world renowned artist's dying wish was for his family to do the one thing that would ensure his legacy for all time—license his name out to a Teenage Mutant Ninja Turtle.

જી03

1972   The California Supreme Court struck down the state's death penalty. With the exception, of course, for the people who were to become victims of the criminals who were now no longer bothered by the existence of the death penalty.

1878   Thomas Edison patented the phonograph, an invention he'd for years gone round and round with trying to perfect.

જી03

1861   Serfdom was abolished in Russia, though to this day it still flourishes along the Hawaiian and California coastlines.

1947   Prussia ceased to exist. Simultaneously, thousands of Prussians shouted en masse, "hey, what the hell?!"

ℰℭ

1792   The Postal Service Act was signed by George Washington, officially creating the United States Post Office. Fittingly, the document took over two weeks to deliver.

1918   The last Carolina parakeet died in captivity at the Cincinnati Zoo. Homesickness, perhaps?

ℰℭ

1986   Nintendo introduced the video game *The Legend of Zelda*. four months and 84 long distance calls to Seattle later, I'd finally shown it who was boss.

1872   The first national convention of the Prohibition Party took place in Columbus, Ohio. They were renowned for their opposition to the sale and consumption of alcohol. In *America*. Guys, perhaps it's time you considered trying a different marketing strategy.

ℰℭ

1630   Indians in Massachusetts introduced the pilgrims to popcorn at Thanksgiving. It was all for naught however, as William Bradford had absentmindedly left their microwave back in England.

☞ *Also on this date: "Miracle on Ice" (1980) The United States Olympic ice hockey team defeated the Soviet Union 4–3. Their virtually impossible accomplishment remains the greatest upset in sports history.* 👉

☞ *Born on this date: George Washington (1732)—first U.S. president, victorious Revolutionary War General. President Washington was renowned for his unquestionable honesty and integrity. In fact, he was endowed with such an honorable character that he was technically unfit to hold public office.* 👉

23

1993   Scientists cloned a sheep using a cell culled from the breast of another. To honor that, they then named the clone after buxom country singer Dolly Parton. At the procedure's conclusion, a grateful scientist expressed his appreciation to the donor with the remark, "hey ewe, thanks for the mammaries."

☜☞

1969   The first scheduled Hovercraft service in Canada took place in Vancouver, though it would still be 16 more years before Marty McFly would upgrade the concept to a Hoverboard.

24

1997   The Australian parliament overturned the world's first euthanasia law, calling their decision to revoke the edict a mercy killing.

☜☞

1942   The *Battle of Los Angeles* took place. It lasted only a few hours though as, being L.A., the participants left after the seventh inning to beat the traffic.

৪০৫৪

1857   The government of the United States ordered the first perforated postage stamps. This was done in an effort to show the constituency that Washington was not in any way afraid to tackle the country's toughest issues.

_____

1913   The 16th Amendment was ratified, creating the Federal Income Tax. Though it was touted by Congress as merely a "temporary" tax, its built-in expiration date was nevertheless set to coincide with the Earth's absorption into the sun.

৪০৫৪

1793   George Washington held the first cabinet meeting as President of the United States. It was delayed half an hour so aides could shuffle around the glasses, plates and Campbell's Soup so as to allow them to all fit in.

_____

1797   The Bank of England issued the first one and two pound notes. They were discontinued though, after a sudden rash of hernias erupted throughout London.

৪০৫৪

1829   Levi Strauss was born in Germany. Throughout his life, it was repeatedly said that he'd always had that entrepreneurial spirit in his jeans. Err, genes.

৪০৫৪

1870   A demonstration of the first pneumatic subway was opened to the public in New York City. For marketing purposes, it was billed as "A Shot in the Dark."

1986   The U.S. Senate allowed its debates to be televised on a trial basis. Over the ensuing years, tens of people have tuned in to watch.

୧୦୯୫

1998   Apple discontinued the development of their Newton computer. It seems that the . . . Hey, wait a second—I just got that. Apple . . . Newton. That's pretty clever. Now I can't even remember the damn joke I was going to write.

୧୦୯୫

1940   Carbon-14 was discovered. Though to date, Carbons 1 through 13 have never been found.

1646   Roger Scott was put on trial in Massachusetts for sleeping in church. During the proceedings, his attorney offered up as a defense that Scott was up all night the previous Saturday taping the St. Louis Rams practice, for use by the New England Patriots coaching staff.

୧୦୯୫

1935   DuPont scientist Wallace Carothers invented Nylon, which instantly caused a large run on stockings.

1960   The comic strip Family Circus debuted. No wonder Billy looks perpetually eight years old. After 50 years, he only is about eight years old. It makes me wish I was born on Leap Year.

୧୦୯୫

1916 The minimum working age for factory, mill, and mine workers was raised in South Carolina from 12 to 14 years old. Though that still sounded somewhat extreme to the public, the governor responded by pointing that out each teen would be given one 15-minute cigarette break.

ଛଠଓଃ

1980 Hartford Whaler Gordie Howe made NHL history by scoring his 800th goal. Look, you should all know that any chance I get to put my Hartford Whalers in this book, I'm damn well going to take it.

MARCH

1642 Present day York, Maine, became the first incorporated city in America, though ironically it was simultaneously listed last, alphabetically.

ଛଠଓଃ

1847 The state of Michigan formally abolished capital punishment, though lowercase punishment is still on the books.

1917 Nicolas II abdicated the Russian throne in favor of his brother, Michael II. Perhaps more interesting is the paternal story behind these two.

ଛଠଓଃ

986 Louis V became King of the Franks and, by default, the Beans.

1933 Mount Rushmore National Memorial was dedicated. Several critics in attendance wrote that the presidents depicted seemed to take themselves too seriously, as they all appeared to be somewhat stone-faced.

ဆၧ

TAKE 2: 1933 Mount Rushmore National Memorial was dedicated. The celebration took an unfortunate turn though when the project's sculptor, Gutzon Borglum, ran cackling insanely off into the night after being informed the third president depicted was supposed to have been Franklin, not Teddy, Roosevelt.

ဆၧ

1634 The first tavern in Boston, Massachusetts opened for business. For those of you who don't live here in New England, I can assure you—it was not the last.

1275 Chinese astronomers observed a total eclipse of the sun. Their glee was short lived however, once they came to the realization that it would be centuries before Bonnie Tyler would be able to paraphrase the event into a hit song.

ဆၧ

1902 In Chicago, Illinois the American Automobile Association (AAA) was established. The biggest hurdle it faced was that membership cost $87 million per customer, the result of there being only four cars on the road in 1902 nationwide.

1872   George Westinghouse patented the air brake. All things being equal, I'd still rather take my chances with a parachute.

৪০৫৪

1958   The Explorer 2 spacecraft was launched, but failed to reach Earth's orbit. An investigation later revealed the slingshot's rubber band wasn't thick enough to create the required velocity.

1899   Bayer registered aspirin as a trademark, though they admitted later that the registration process had been one major headache.

৪০৫৪

1460   In trade, Portugal gave the Canary Islands to Castile, which Castile decided to take only after Portugal agreed to throw in a year's supply of old newspapers.

1983   The Nashville Network (TNN) began broadcasting, finally giving the country what it had long and collectively cried out for—a place to watch reruns of Hee Haw and The Dukes of Hazzard.

৪০৫৪

1876   Alexander Graham Bell received a patent for the telephone. I guess one could say that the patent was a ringing endorsement for it.

1979 Philips publicly demonstrated the compact disc for the first time. When a reporter asked just how much of an improvement the CD was over 8-track cassettes, he was answered, "Roughly about the same upgrade as a Ferrari would be to that meat covered thing Fred Flintstone drove with his feet."

ಬಿಂ

1854 United States Commodore Matthew Perry completed his second landing in Japan. According to his handlers though, he also traveled under the alias Chandler Bing.

ಬಿಂ

1936 Daytona Beach Road Course held their first oval stock car race. It went much, much better than the triangle stock car race they'd tried first.

1765 After a public campaign by Voltaire, Parisian judges exonerated Jean Calas, whom they'd already executed for killing his own son. Responded Calas's ghost, "An exoneration? Cool. However if I don't sound too appreciative, that'd be because I'm still freaking dead."

ಬಿಂ

1996 Comedian George Burns died at age 100, leaving producers of the planned blockbuster comedy sequel, *Oh, God, Book IV* severely in the lurch.

1965   Neil Simon's play *The Odd Couple* opened on Broadway, starring British theoretical physicist Stephen Hawking, and actress Jessica Simpson.

෨෬

1975   In England, a patent was granted for canine spectacles. Though it doesn't specify why, I can only guess that this was Britain's first attempt to train seeing-eye dogs.

෨෬

1992   Natalie Cole and Color Me Badd won at the Soul Train music awards, with the latter losing out later in the subsequent Spelling Bee competition.

1997   Former Beatle Paul McCartney was knighted. Though privately, he still complained to friends about how the chain mail scratched his guitar.

෨෬

1970   The album *Déjà vu* by Crosby, Stills, Nash and Young was released. Though many customers reported they'd had the oddest feeling that they'd already bought it before.

1970   The U.S. lowered the voting age from 21 to 18, thus overnight giving thousands more young Americans the opportunity to blow off the same elections that their elders did.

৪০৫

1912   Juliette Gordon Low founded the Girl Guides, which later became the Girl Scouts of America. Years later, she admitted the whole thing was just a scam to corner the country's eccentric cookie market.

1781   German astronomer William Herschel discovered Uranus, apparently after probing for hours.

৪০৫

1991   Exxon dejectedly paid $1 billion in fines and cleanup costs for the *Exxon Valdez* oil spill. This scuttled their original plan, which was to send a two-man custodian crew up to Alaska with four cases of Bounty paper towels.

1923   Peter Parker performed the world's first play-by-play radio broadcast of a professional hockey game. He'd wanted to make a career of it, but was subsequently bitten by a radioactive spider and thus forced into a life of fighting crime.

৪০৫

1935   Shirley Temple left her handprints at the famous Grauman's Chinese Theatre. Originally scheduled to be footprints, no one had thought to warn her about the nearby extension cords used for the camera equipment.

1920   Maine was admitted to the Union as part of the Missouri Compromise. Overnight, the U.S. population skyrocketed by 13.

᙮

1672 Charles II of England issued the Royal Declaration of Indulgence, setting a precedent that has been enthusiastically followed by governing bodies and heads of virtually every other country in the three plus centuries since.

1916 The United States and Canada signed a migratory bird treaty. Of course if this were done present day, both the U.S. and Canadian birds would have to spend weeks just waiting to receive their passports.

᙮

1621 The Mohegan Indian Samoset visited the settlers of Plymouth Colony, greeting them with, "Welcome, Englishmen! My name is Samoset. Can I get you anything?" To which the lead pilgrim replied, "Sure, thanks. We'll take some corn, some squash, a couple of pumpkins, a few turkeys and the entire Eastern Seaboard."

Today is St. Patrick's Day. On this date, St. Patrick drove all the snakes out of Ireland. Some of them went north, some went south, and some ended up running for public office.

᙮

1845 The rubber band was patented. While still in the planning stages, many detractors thought the whole concept itself was a real stretch.

1931 Schick marketed the first electric razor, creating a huge buzz throughout the industry.

৪৩০৪

TAKE 2: 1931 Schick marketed the first electric razor. Up until that time they'd been just scraping by.

৪৩০৪

2003 Sign Language was recognized as an official British language. They'd have recognized it sooner, but it took them longer than expected to figure out how to incorporate the accent.

1979 The U.S. House of Representatives began broadcasting its daily proceedings on C-SPAN, as insomniacs throughout the country rejoiced in their new cure.

৪৩০৪

1931 Nevada legalized gambling. The result was unexpected, as local bookmakers had put the odds on its passage at 20–1.

1916 Albert Einstein published his General Theory of Relativity. When asked to elaborate, he responded that it should've been obvious that he wasn't going to be getting into any specifics.

৪৩০৪

1954   The first ever newspaper vending machine was put into use. It forced that paper's writers to ultimately leave all of their thinking inside the box.

2000   The Supreme Court ruled the government lacked authority to regulate tobacco as an addictive drug. A good call too, as there's never really been any evidence to suggest nicotine is any more addictive to smokers than say, oxygen, is.

ಬಂಗ

1980   Jimmy Carter announced a U.S. boycott of the 1980 Summer Olympics in Moscow to protest the Soviet Invasion of Afghanistan. Upon hearing this, a response was issued which read: *in light of the news that we will apparently be denied the opportunity to compete against the West in the uneven parallel bars competition, we have no choice but to commence an immediate withdrawal of our troops from Afghanistan.* Then they all had a good laugh and returned to their regularly scheduled invasion.

1882   Congress outlawed polygamy. In a related story, Congress then immediately moved their offices to Utah.

ಬಂಗ

1933   During Prohibition, Franklin Roosevelt signed a measure making beer containing 3.2% alcohol legal. Many still complained, reasoning that such beer might as well have some mint flavor added and called *Scope*.

1775 Virginia's Patrick Henry delivered his famous "Give me liberty, or give me death!" speech. He later agreed that the line as originally written: *Give me liberty, or give me a somewhat moderately unpleasant case of gingivitis!* wouldn't have had quite the same enduring impact on American history.

෮෬

1857 Elisha Otis unveiled his first elevator on Broadway in New York City. To the press, Otis hailed his contraption as completely safe. Though that was indeed true, he neglected to mention that he'd installed it into a one story building.

1786 The British government prohibited trade between British North America and the United States. As a result, Americans were suddenly and unexpectedly left with nothing to put on there pancakes.

෮෬

1975 The Canadian Parliament passed an act which elevated the beaver to Canada's official symbol, though only after the bucktoothed rodent barely beat out bottle of Labatt's in the voting.

1409 The Council of Pisa opened. Apparently, they were all sitting on the same side of the tower.

෮෬

1996 The redesigned $100 bill went into circulation. So for one day at least, it literally was all about the Benjamins.

1911 Playwright Tennessee Williams was born in Mississippi. Evidently, Rand McNally was not on the southern required reading list at the time.

৪০৫৪

1804 President Thomas Jefferson was presented with a mammoth loaf of bread. In tribute to Jefferson, contemporary politicians keep this beloved tradition alive by accepting mammoth amounts of bread from lobbyists to this very day.

৪০৫৪

1934 The first driving test to obtain licenses began in the United Kingdom, while here in America, Massachusetts residents are evidently still waiting for their qualifying tests to be given.

1906 The Alpine Club of Canada for Mountaineering was founded on the prairies of Winnipeg, Manitoba. Which I guess is sort of like founding the American Surfing Club in Wichita, Kansas.

৪০৫৪

1998 The Food and Drug Administration approved Pfizer's drug Viagra to fight impotence. Since then however, the popular drug has faced some pretty stiff competition.

1797 Nathaniel Briggs of New Hampshire patented the washing machine, calling his invention the Rock and Stream 2000.

ഇഗ

1802 Heinrich Olbers discovered only the second asteroid known to man. At that pace it's no wonder it took Atari so long to debut.

1806 Construction was authorized on the Cumberland Road, which was to become the first federal highway in the U.S. That construction is currently scheduled to be completed sometime late next year.

ഇഗ

1929 Herbert Hoover had the first telephone installed in the Oval Office, which he then used to score tons of free pizza, knowing full well that Domino's would never be able to get through to the Oval in 30 minutes or less.

1842 Anesthesia was used during an operation for the first time. I can't help but wonder though just how pissed off the guy who'd had an appendectomy the day before was.

ഇഗ

1867 Seward's Folly occurred, as U.S. Secretary of State William Seward was lambasted for spending over $7 million to purchase Alaska. After months of incessant criticism, a frustrated Seward finally screamed to a reporter that enough was enough. He explained that we had needed a place to hold the Iditarod, and now we'd gotten one. End of Story.

1930   The Motion Pictures Production Code was instituted, imposing strict guidelines on the treatment of sex, crime, religion and violence in motion pictures. Their first rating was a PG-29.

଼ଓଌ

1967   Jimi Hendrix burned his guitar in London. Evidently, the performance was a flaming success.

☞   *Born on this date: Gordie Howe (1928)—Right Wing, New England/Hartford Whalers (1977–1980) "Mr. Hockey."* ☜

☞   *Born on this date: Christopher Walken (1943)—American actor; listed here for virtually no other reason than his acting style is so often freaking hysterical.* ☜

APRIL _____ 1

1918   Britain established the Royal Air Force. They found that the toughest part was getting the tiara to balance on top of the cockpit window.

଼ଓଌ

1929   The yo-yo was introduced by Louie Marx, who appeared at the press conference to be all wound up about it.

☞   *Also on this date: Today is April Fool's Day. There are so many out there lately though, it's probably time to give this holiday its own month. (Not for you, however. You're cool. Seriously. I was talking about other people entirely.)*

1987 Congress allowed individual states to increase the speed limit. In stating that decree, Congress had clearly failed to take my aunt into consideration.

৪০৻

1877 The first Easter egg roll was held on White House lawn. In a related story: later that same day, the first omelet brunch was held on the White House lawn.

1986 The U.S. national debt reached $2,000,000,000,000; it was a time period that's now referred to by some economists as "the good old days."

৪০৻

1924 Marlon Brando was born in Omaha, Nebraska. He passed away 400 lb. later in Los Angeles, California.

1581 Sir Francis Drake was knighted by Queen Elizabeth I for circumnavigating the globe. So? What's the circumference of the average globe—4 feet, tops?

৪০৻

1862 The Battle of Yorktown began, causing the entire town to undergo an enormous, collective case of déjà vu.

৪০৻

1964 The Beatles occupied the top five spots on the U.S. Billboard singles chart. Since then, only Madonna has shown the flexibility to assume that many positions at once.

456 St. Patrick returned to Ireland from England. Though he claimed to have had a pleasant trip back, reports recently unearthed from that the time indicate that he still looked a little green.

§✂∞

1887 British historian Lord Acton wrote, *All power tends to corrupt and absolute power corrupts absolutely.* You know, it's fairly remarkable that a 19th century English writer could be so prophetic with regard to contemporary American politics.

1980 Post-it Notes were introduced. 3M inventor Art Fry was credited with having a real "stick-to-itiveness" on the project.

§✂∞

1987 Paul Sahli juggled a soccer ball nonstop for over 14 hours. Evidently, he was really on the ball that day.

§✂∞

1954 Swanson sold its first TV Dinner. I guess one could say that this historic moment is frozen in time.

Today Thanksgiving Day is observed in Canada. Today people from Nova Scotia to British Columbia will gather together and celebrate with turkey and mashed potatoes. Except, not really. In actuality our Canadian friends observe Thanksgiving in October. I'm simply demonstrating that you shouldn't believe everything you read.

ဆလ

1983   In Egypt, what was believed to be the oldest human skeleton was discovered, though it turned out to just be a vacationing Larry King.

1766   The first fire escape was patented, consisting of a wicker basket on a pulley and chain. This might not have been such a good idea, however, as wicker is made out of plants and wood, and fire is made out of fire.

ဆလ

1986   Clint Eastwood was elected mayor of Carmel-by-the-Sea, California, whose citizens had decided the time had come to bring in Dirty Harry after years of living with villainous litterbugs and nefarious jaywalkers.

1953   TV Guide published its premiere issue and finally, at long last, the viewing public was able to stop wasting its time surfing through the three channels that existed in 1953.

ဆလ

1945   The NFL required players to wear long stockings, evidently never anticipating how far Joe Namath would take things to the next level.

1995   New York City banned smoking in restaurants that seated 35 or more patrons. Apparently if you prefer quiet little out-of-the-way eateries, you're stuck with a side of carcinogens, for all New York cares.

෩෬

1938   New York made syphilis tests a mandatory prerequisite to obtain a marriage license, unless, evidently, you were marrying more than 35 people.

෩෬

1865   The last photograph was taken of Abraham Lincoln while he was still living, though cinematography experts reported that Lincoln came off as looking rather two dimensional.

1984   Challenger astronauts completed the first satellite repair in space. They then huddled up and after a long discussion, decided it would be easier on them just to switch to cable TV.

෩෬

1921   Iowa became the first state to impose a cigarette tax. In retaliation, Virginia immediately imposed a tax on corn.

1811   The first U.S. colonists on the Pacific coast arrived at Cape Disappointment, Washington, content that at least they knew in advance not really to expect all that much.

෩෬

1960   White Sox owner Bill Veeck unveiled his Exploding Scoreboard at Chicago's Comisky Park. Originally built for use at Wrigley Field to celebrate World Series victories, the Cubs ultimately sold it off to their crosstown rival in the hope that it might get used some day.

1741 The Dutch people protested the bad quality of bread. Huh, of all the things that could've gotten a rise out of them. I guess one could say that they'd had a "yeast insurrection." Ok, I'll stop now.

ೞೞ

1984 Pete Rose became the first National Leaguer to reach 4,000 hits. Oh, you bet he did … and so did he.

☞ *Also on this date: (1997) The last NHL game was played in Hartford, Connecticut, as the Hartford Whalers defeated the Tampa Bay Lightning 2–1. Today is also known in Hartford as The Day The Earth Stood Still.*

1881 The *Four Dead in Five Seconds Gunfight* erupted in El Paso, Texas. It literally was over almost before it began.

ೞೞ

1828 The first edition of Noah Webster's *American Dictionary of the English Language* was published. Determined not to be outdone, a few years later Webster's cousin Jeremiah Wikipedia published the first interactive online encyclopedia.

1865 Abraham Lincoln passed away in Washington, D.C. In 1912, the RMS Titanic sank in the North Atlantic Ocean and—it's tax day. Yet for some reason, people are still worried about the 13th.

ೞೞ

1990 Actress Greta Garbo died at age 84. Her last words were—as you might have guessed—nothing.

1943 Dr. Albert Hoffman discovered the psychedelic effects of LSD. He then voluntarily continued his "research" until 1956.

୫୦ରଃ

1856 James Douglas declared that all gold found in British Columbia was to become property of the British Crown. Douglas held the official government title of *Secretary of the Royal Canadian Department of Bwa-haha, You Worthless Peasants! It's Ours! Every Damn Ounce Is All Ours!*

୫୦ରଃ

1956 The first solar powered radios went on sale. The radios flopped however, as they were advertised under the unfortunate slogan, "Tuck 'em away for a rainy day."

1997 115-year-old John Bell received a new pacemaker. In an effort to showcase their generosity to the public, his HMO threw in a lifetime money back guarantee.

୫୦ରଃ

1967 In Ontario, Canada, Roland Michener took office as the third Canadian-born Governor-General. I don't know; maybe it's just me ... but I guess I just figured that they'd pretty much all be Canadian.

1955   The first *Walk/Don't Walk* lighted street signals were installed. They were modified versions, as the initial *Walk/Don't Walk/Break Dance* signs were simply causing too many crosswalks accidents.

৵ৎ

1963   Dr. James Campbell performed the first human nerve transplant, henceforth dooming his patient to a lifetime of "Hey! You've got a lot of nerve" jokes.

৵ৎ

1968   San Francisco's Old Hall of Justice was demolished, leaving Batman and the Green Lantern with nowhere to hold their northern California meetings.

৵ৎ

1991   The U.S. Census Bureau said that it failed to count about 63 million people in the 1990 census. I think the obvious question is, how did they know how many they'd missed without counting them?

1692   Bridget Bishop went on trial for Witchcraft in Salem. If she *was* guilty, who could blame her? History shows that in Massachusetts, no matter how heinous your crime, you're still at least able to run for Senate.

৵ৎ

1775 The Revolutionary War began in earnest with after the firing of the *The Shot Heard 'Round the World* on the town green in Lexington, Massachusetts around 5 a.m., as 50 Minutemen attempted to block a detachment of 700 British soldiers. It's probably a safe assumption that the green's tavern was serving alcohol earlier that night.

20

1940 RCA publicly demonstrated their new electron microscope. Those gathered around to watch were amazed that, at long last, they'd have the technology to see the morals of their local politicians.

ꙮ

1775 The British began their siege of Boston. It ultimately ended in failure however, as unbeknownst to the British, the Patriots coaching staff had taped their pre-siege warm ups. (*Author's Note: Yes, yes ... I'm aware that this is my second joke at the Patriot's expense; but you see I'm from Hartford, Connecticut; and if you are too, you understand. Carry on.*)

21

1910 Author Mark Twain died at age 74. It appears that this time at least, the reports of his death were not quite so exaggerated.

ꙮ

1918 Baron Manfred von Richthofen, the German flying ace known famously as the *Red Baron,* was killed in action during World War I. Said Snoopy at his debriefing, "Hey, he had it coming."

හිංග

1993 Brazil voted against a monarchy. How strong a monarchy would it have been anyway, if you could vote against it?

1969 The first human eye transplant was performed. That must have been a sight to see.

හිංග

TAKE 2: 1969 The first human eye transplant was performed. That must have been a sight for sore eyes.

හිංග

1906 A new rule put the umpires in sole charge of all game baseballs. It sort of makes you wonder who they left in charge of them prior.

1564 William Shakespeare was born on the exact day he was to die on 52 years later. It seems that in death, as in life, he was really into bookends.

හිංග

1972 The surface of the Moon was investigated by the Apollo 16 astronauts. The results of which revealed the disappointing news that the American dairy industry was still going to have to continue producing cheese.

1950 President Harry Truman denied there were any communists in the U.S. government. Across the Atlantic Ocean however, Soviet Premier Joseph Stalin sheepishly admitted that there may be a few of them in Russia's.

&⟨⟩

1800 Congress approved a bill establishing the Library of Congress, then for good measure approved the Bathroom, Pantry, and Breakfast Nook of Congress, too.

1901 New York became the first state to require license plates. Still, the four registered drivers in the state at the time somehow ended up waiting in line for three hours at the DMV, anyway.

&⟨⟩

1792 Highwayman Nicolas Jacques Pelletier became the first person under French law to be executed by guillotine. He told the trial judge that he just wanted to experience a slice of life, to which the judge responded, "Ironically, now it'll be just the opposite."

1962 NASA's spacecraft Ranger 4 crashed into the moon. I'd warned them not to let my aunt drive; but no, they were all like, *hey, it's space. What the hell can she hit?* They aren't laughing now.

&⟨⟩

1564 William Shakespeare was christened. The priest had been so late in arriving that for a while, no one was really quite sure whether the ceremony was to be, or not to be.

1872 Samuel Morse, inventor of both Morse code and the telegraph, passed away. When asked what should be played at the funeral, his wife requested *Taps*.

༄༅

1962 The U.S. performed an atmospheric nuclear test at Christmas Island. Now at least we know how all of those toys became misfits.

1992 The Department of Agriculture unveiled a pyramid-shaped diet chart, though the new one still contained almost two-thirds the calories of the leading chart.

༄༅

1914 W. H. Carrier patented the air conditioner. I guess you could say he was looking to create one cool customer.

1553 A Flemish woman introduced the practice of starching linen into England, thereby causing an obesity epidemic for British bed sheets—which were suddenly overloaded with carbohydrates.

෯෬

1429   Joan of Arc entered the besieged city of Orleans to lead a victory over the English. She then moved to Arcadia, California, and spent the rest of her youth claiming to see God everywhere.

1772   John Clais patented the first scale, an invention that ultimately carried a lot of weight within the community.

෯෬

1952   Mr. Potato Head became the first toy advertised on television. Conveniently, the spot was also able to double as the first political advertisement.

☞   *Also in April: Arbor Day. I hope you read this reminder early enough that you've had time to avoid the crowds and were able to get all of your Arbor Day shopping done.*

MAY_____ **1**

1751   The first cricket match was played in America, though afterward they evidently had some difficulty getting them all back into the cages.

෯෬

1844   Samuel Morse sent the first telegraphic message. It read: *Would somebody please invent the damn telephone? My fingers are killing me!*

1972   Buddy Baker became the first stock car racer to finish a 500 mile race in less than three hours. When asked how he accomplished the incredible feat, Baker stated it wasn't intentional, just that he'd drunk a gallon of water beforehand.

ℰ◯ℭ

1519   Leonardo da Vinci passed away. Reportedly, his last words were: Wait—the eyebrows! I forgot the eyebrows!

1938   The Vatican recognized Franco-Spain. In response, Chef Boyardee recognized Franco-American.

ℰ◯ℭ

1952   Lt. Colonels Joseph Fletcher and William Benedict successfully landed a plane on the North Pole. The feat was short lived unfortunately, as they quickly lost their balance and fell off.

1984   A fly ball hit by Dave Kingman into Minnesota's Metrodome roof never came down, finally disproving *Blood, Sweat and Tears* once and for all.

ℰ◯ℭ

1846   Michigan put an end to the death penalty, though all the prisoners died anyway. Eventually.

1640   King Charles I of England disbanded the Short Parliament. All members over 5′7″, however, were allowed to stay.

                   ଽଠଓଷ

1865   In North Bend, Ohio, the first train robbery in the United States took place, though it was never fully explained how the perpetrators were able to walk off carrying an entire train.

                   ଽଠଓଷ

1921   The *Brighton Gazette* was published as a miniature newspaper. I guess it wasn't too much trouble for readers to spot the small print.

1940   John Steinbeck was awarded the Pulitzer Prize for his novel *The Grapes of Wrath*. It was later turned into a low budget horror film featuring wronged fruit on a mission of vengeance entitled, *The Wrath of Grapes*.

                   ଽଠଓଷ

1851   Linus Yale received a patent for his Yale padlock, an idea he'd kept under lock and key for many years prior.

1992   Guitarist John Frusciante left the Red Hot Chili Peppers. That's pretty much it for news. I guess this is one example of why you never hear May 7 referred to as "Siete de Mayo."

                   ଽଠଓଷ

1934   The world's largest pearl—weighing in at 14lbs.—was found in the Philippines. That's cool, sure; but I'd rather know the size of the damn oyster.

1900   250 grave robbers were shot to death. On a positive note, the shooters didn't have too far to carry them.

૪ОСЗ

1877   The first Westminster Dog Show was held. Unfortunately, the winner turned out to be a real bitch.

☞ *Born on this date: Harry S. Truman (1884)—33rd U.S. president, arguably the best Democrat ever to serve as president.* ☜

1502   Christopher Columbus left for his final journey to the New World, pledging as he left that this time, he was going to find the damn cinnamon.

૪ОСЗ

1092   The Lincoln Cathedral was consecrated. Though curiously, Mrs. Lincoln was nowhere to be found.

૪ОСЗ

1962   A laser beam was successfully bounced off the Moon for the first time, and although technically historic, the kid was given a detention, anyway.

1497   Italian cartographer Amerigo Vespucci left for his first voyage to the New World. If ever there was a guy who missed the boat on naming rights, this was probably him.

೮೧೮೩

1775   Fort Ticonderoga was taken from the British by Americans Ethan Allen and Benedict Arnold, who then spent decades there turning out high quality, #2 lead pencils.

೮೧೮೩

1931   Golf ball sized hail fell in NJ. In a cool quirk of fate, it was followed up by 9 iron sized snowflakes.

1960   The first contraceptive pill was made available, creating a nationwide barrier that was virtually impregnable.

೮೧೮೩

1858   Minnesota was admitted as our 32nd State. Overnight, our Olympic ice hockey rankings skyrocketed.

೮೧೮೩

1947   B.F. Goodrich announced the development of tubeless tire, despite a strong and bitter protest from the sledding industry.

1986   A bicycle was pedaled at 65 mph. My best guess is that wherever that cyclist started from, it was all downhill from there.

ಬೃೊ

1963   Bob Dylan walked off Ed Sullivan Show. He did try to explain his reasoning, but unfortunately no one could make out what he was trying to say.

1204   The Fourth Crusade sacked Constantinople, bringing it to within five of Bruce Smith's all-time record.

ಬೃೊ

1902   James C. Penney opened his first store in Kemmerer, Wyoming. He opened more soon after, once it occurred to him that business might be better if he located a few stores where even a trace amount of human existence might be found.

ಬೃೊ

1950   Diner's Club issued its first credit cards, but missed a huge opportunity when they couldn't strike a deal to become the official card of the San Diego Chargers.

1878   Vaseline was sold for the first time. As a courtesy, five million cases were given away to those most in need of it—America's middle class.

ಬೃೊ

1991   The world's largest burrito was made, weighing in at 1,126 lb. It was nothing though compared to the size of the Tums they created to go with it.

1918   The Finnish Civil War ended. I guess you could say it was ... finished.

&❧&

1918   Walter Johnson pitched and won a 1–0 game that lasted 18 innings, adding to a resume that proved him to be one of the most productive Senators ever to work in Washington.

1965   Franco-American introduced SpaghettiOs, thus setting French cuisine back to, roughly, the dawn of time.

&❧&

1924   Blitzen, Oregon, reached 108° Fahrenheit. After that publicity debacle, no other reindeer would ever lend his name to any town south of Vancouver.

1775   The American Continental Congress banned trade with Canada, stating that we already had more maple syrup then we knew what to do with.

&❧&

1620   The first merry-go-round was seen at a fair, prompting one woman in attendance to comment, "Now there's a horse of a different color."

1881   Frederick Douglass was appointed Recorder of Deeds for Washington D.C. and, not surprisingly, developed Carpel Tunnel within his first hour on the job.

&❧&

1673   Louis Joliet and Jacques Marquette began exploring the Mississippi River. The journal Joliet left behind indicated that, after careful examination, he found it to be rather wet.

1897   Bram Stoker's *Dracula* was published. One review at the time described it as having a plot that "struck you with the force of a stake through the heart."

ဆာၚ

1631   John Winthrop became the first governor of Massachusetts. After taking the oath of office, he told an aide that he suddenly had an inexplicable urge to tax somebody for something.

1536   Anne Boleyn, wife of Henry VIII of England, was beheaded for adultery, causing Hester Prynne to quickly rethink her vocal opposition to wearing that scarlet letter.

ဆာၚ

1848   The first department store opened. It was a major flop, as virtually no one at that time was in the market to buy a department.

1980   Drummer Peter Criss quit the band Kiss, and in the process almost single-handedly bankrupted Cover Girl.

ဆာၚ

1892 George Sampson patented the clothes dryer toward the end of the 19th century. He marketed it under the name, *Fresh Air.*

21

1936 Sada Abe was arrested after wandering the Tokyo streets for days with her dead lover's severed genitals in her hand. That woman must've had some balls to pull a stunt like that.

ꕥ

1943 The fastest nine inning American League baseball game took place as Chicago beat Washington over only 89 minutes. I wonder how that ... oh, right—no commercials.

ꕥ

1804 The Lewis and Clark Expedition began as Clark shouted out that he would race Lewis to the Pacific, and then abruptly took off.

22

1992 After almost 30 years, Johnny Carson hosted NBC's Tonight Show for the last time; consequently, a directionless Ed McMahon had nothing left to do but fake laugh heartily at the antics of the cleaning crew.

ꕥ

1906 The Wright Brothers received a patent for their "Flying Machine." A week later they received patents for a three-peanut snack bag and watered down Scotch.

1785 Benjamin Franklin announced he had invented bifocals. Franklin followed up the announcement by stating that his creation was the culmination of a great lifelong vision.

౸౸

1929 The first nonstop Winnipeg-to-Edmonton flight was incredibly made in less than seven hours. When the passengers disembarked and looked around however, no one could figure out what the rush was for.

1931 The first air-conditioned train was installed on the B&O Railroad. Hopefully, it helped things out a bit.

౸౸

1899 The first auto repair shop opened in Boston, Massachusetts. I'm just trying to imagine how high an estimate to fix a car would've been from this place, at a time with zero competition.

౸౸

1844 Samuel Morse tapped out the first telegraph message, *What hath God wrought?* To which God tapped back, *Sammy, you ain't seen nothing yet.*

1986 In Florida, a 95-year-old woman achieved a hole in one. My guess is that she timed the windmill just right.

౸౸

1963 Early Wynn won his 300th game, as it appears evident that he won a few late ones, too.

1930   The Supreme Court ruled that buying liquor did not violate the Constitution. The only catch was that drinking it, did.

෨෮෮

1998   The Supreme Court ruled that the famous Ellis Island is located not mainly in New York, but primarily in New Jersey. Ah, well. To the victor go the soils.

1997   The first all-female team reached the North Pole. In an unrelated story, also on this date in 1997, Santa Claus announced a lengthy, previously unscheduled sabbatical.

෨෮෮

1919   Charles Strite patented the pop-up toaster. It took a few more modifications however for him to get it to stay in place.

1503   England and Scotland signed the Treaty of Everlasting Peace, which lasted only 10 years. If you're looking to get either country a birthday gift, perhaps a dictionary might prove useful.

෨෮෮

2006   Barry Bonds hit his 715th home run, passing Babe Ruth's all time record. Bonds total turned out to be a number as authentic and genuine as any that were found on Al Capone's tax returns.

1790   Rhode Island officially became our 13th state. They then immediately unveiled their new state motto, *Rhode Island: Connecticut's Toenail,* which had narrowly edged out the runner up, *Rhode Island: Not Really An Island, But Close Enough.*

৪০৫৪

1942   Bing Crosby recorded *White Christmas* in Los Angeles, which kind of seems akin to him recording *Mele Kalikimaka* in Buffalo, New York.

1933   A patent was granted for the installation of invisible glass and finally, at long last, Wonder Woman's plane was completed.

৪০৫৪

Today   Today is former Red Sox outfielder Manny Ramirez's birthday. I'm sure someone will let him know.

৪০৫৪

1868   Memorial Day was observed for the first time when two women in Mississippi placed flowers on both Confederate and Union graves. It certainly seems that there was lot those two women could've taught the rest of us.

1984   Daniel Greenblatt won the 57th National Spelling Bee by correctly spelling the word "luge." Seriously? I hope he had to at least spell something like *supercalifragilisticexpialidocious* to get to that final round.

ɛɔdʒ

1943   The *Archie* comic strip was first broadcast on radio. Now how did that work, exactly?

ɛɔdʒ

1930   Iconic screen legend Clint Eastwood was born in San Francisco, California, as his mom went ahead and made his day.

☞   *Also in May: Manchester, Connecticut, was incorporated (1823)—What can I tell you? It's my hometown.*

JUNE _____ 1

1843   It snowed in Buffalo, New York. Huh, it appears Vanessa Williams was right, after all.

ɛɔdʒ

1494   Friar John Cor recorded the first known batch of Scotch whiskey, after 700 men lined up and voluntarily confirmed it for him.

☞   *Born on this date: Morgan Freeman (1937)—American actor. In my opinion, he's one our best.*

_____ 2

1774   England passed the "Quartering Act," which required American colonists to use their own homes to provide shelter to British troops. This act, among others, led to the Colonials passing the "Screw You, Parliament" act of 1776, in which the Continental Congress declared independence, then showed the England the door.

෨෬

1988   Rageshree Ramachandran won the 61st National Spelling Bee, evidently after she was narrowly able to correctly spell her own name.

1856   Cullen Whipple patented the screw machine, which was then immediately purchased by the petroleum industry for use on the American people in perpetuity.

෨෬

1889   The coast to coast Canadian Pacific Railway was completed. Regrettably, no one realized till after the last spike was driven that they had built it in the wrong direction—from the Vancouver coast to the coast of Japan.

1974   The Cleveland Indians "10 Cent Beer Night Promotion" went haywire after the conduct of drunken fans caused the game to be forfeited. You can't really blame the promotions department though. Really, who could've seen that coming?

෨෬

1992   The United States Postal Service announced that America had voted to use the young Elvis on its new stamps, effectively marking the old Elvis version Return to Sender.

1957   New York narcotics investigator Dr. Herbert Berger urged the AMA to investigate use of stimulating drugs by athletes. This proved once and for all that the Yankees should not have lost the '57 World Series to the Milwaukee Braves, who were obviously under the influence back then of ... well, caffeine, I'm sure.

ဆၢ

1995   Bose–Einstein Condensate was created. And thus, the first kick-ass compact stereo with the ability to perform quantum mechanics was born.

1799   Founding Father Patrick Henry passed away in Virginia. Ironically he was given liberty, and then given death anyway.

ဆၢ

1882   Henry Seely patented the electric iron, though he told close friends he wasn't able to get through the process without a few wrinkles.

☞   *Also on this date: D-Day (1944)—World War II: Massive amphibious invasion by Allied troops at Normandy. I'd like to take a moment to honor the enormous sacrifice made that day by so many.* ☜

1557   England declared war on France. It was their right, as France had declared war first on England the last time, after which the countries agreed that simply alternating between the two would be the fairest way to do it for all of their other wars going forward.

෨෬

1955   The quiz show, *$64,000 Question* premiered on CBS. The first winning contestant eventually found out that the answer was: *Yes—it is all considered taxable income.*

1829   In Liverpool, the first United Kingdom municipal swimming pool not located in London, opened. By all accounts, it created a real splash throughout the community.

෨෬

1896   The first car was stolen. In 1896? What'd they do—take it right out of Henry Ford's garage?

1822   Charles Graham patented false teeth, thus leaving the toothpick industry with no bones to pick with him.

෨෬

1943   U.S. income tax deductions directly from workers paychecks were authorized. This had the benefit of giving Americans who desired to maintain their virginity the opportunity to do so, while simultaneously allowing them to feel just what it was like to get screwed.

1935   Alcoholics Anonymous was founded in Akron, Ohio by William G. Wilson and Dr. Robert Smith. Well sure, it's a great organization, but I really think those two may need a refresher on the definition of anonymity.

෨෬

1990   Burger King began using Newman's Own Salad Dressing, leaving Paul miffed that he was then forced to repeatedly eat his salad plain. (*Author's Note: Yeah, I know that joke sucked. But I can do worse. Please see below.*)

ଏଠାଓ

1947   Saab produced its first automobile, literally creating a Saab story. (*Author's Note: Told you.*)

1966   Simon and Garfunkel's hit *I Am A Rock,* peaked at #3 on the music chart. I still can't figure out how Cialis missed out on licensing that one.

ଏଠାଓ

1964   Queen Elizabeth ordered the Beatles to attend her birthday party—and they did. This item finally enabled me to fully comprehend what is meant by the phrase *power to the nth degree.*

1962   Three convict used only spoons to dig their way out of Alcatraz prison. After being recaptured, they explained to police that they hadn't wanted to escape, but rather they were trying a new Betty Crocker recipe that called for 3 tablespoons of sheet rock.

ଏଠାଓ

1792   George Vancouver discovered the site of Vancouver, British Columbia. Admittedly, it was an amazing coincidence.

1920   The United States Postal Service ruled that children may not be sent by Parcel Post. Now I'm just curious here; was it is a close vote?

ಬಂಡ

1930   The first nudist colony opened. Guests were encouraged to attend with only the bare essentials.

1900   Hawaii officially became a U.S. territory, as we shrewdly made the first bold move in our clandestine effort to corner the world's Macadamia nut market.

ಬಂಡ

1775   The United States Army was founded. Thirty seconds later 17-year-old high school student Adam Aaronson was called five separate times by the same military recruiter.

1887   Carlisle Graham—for the second time—survived going over Niagara Falls in a barrel. When asked how he felt about his accomplishment, Graham simply called it just another drop in the bucket.

ಬಂಡ

1992   During a spelling bee, Dan Quayle misspelled the word potato, spelling it *potatoe.* He later explained his error, stating he'd forgotten it was O before E, except after T.

ಬಂಡ

1911 IBM was incorporated. Soon after, they unveiled their first mass-produced consumer product, the electric abacus.

1774 The formation of Harrodsburg, Kentucky, occurred, providing irrefutable proof once and for all that June 16, loosely translated, means *Slow news day.*

ഇ○൫

1784 Holland forbade the wearing of orange clothes, instantly costing Syracuse University any shot they had at recruiting for their 1784 freshman class highly touted Dutch quarterback Aachie Janssen.

1994 O.J. Simpson was arrested and charged in the slayings of his ex-wife and her friend, after a car chase that went on for so long that by the time they'd caught him, he was already eligible for parole.

ഇ○൫

1775 The Revolutionary War Battle of Bunker Hill took place, though it was actually fought on nearby Breed's Hill. If you weren't aware of that it's ok; virtually no graduate of an American high school knows it, either.

1812 The United States declared war on Great Britain for the second time in 36 years. The big screen movie account of this war was entitled, *Independence Day II: Asses Re-kicked.*

ഇ○൫

1948 Columbia unveiled a new, long playing 33⅓ phonograph record. Sony's attempt to trump them and cash in the next year with its new Phonograph Walkman, however, came up well short.

1910 The first Father's Day was celebrated in Spokane, Washington. Apparently, fathers in all other U.S. cities could go screw.

ഇറ

1981 The heaviest known orange, about 5½ lb., was exhibited. One reporter at the scene called covering it "without question, the juiciest story of my career."

1967 Boxer Muhammad Ali was convicted in Houston, Texas, for his refusal to be drafted into the Viet Nam war. The conviction was later overturned in a unanimous, three-judge decision.

ഇറ

1990 The asteroid Eureka was discovered, evidently named after the first thing shouted out by its discovering astronomer.

1981 Donald Fagan and Walter Becker quit Steely Dan. It makes you wonder who was left, as this was roughly akin to Hall and Oates quitting Hall and Oates.

ഇറ

1779 Spain declared war on England, though oddly enough, it had nothing to do with soccer.

1969 The Cuyahoga River caught fire, an event that served as catalyst to a crackdown on the river's pollution. You think? Listen Cleveland, I'm no tree hugger, but if you're tossing away so much junk that it causes a body of water to spontaneously combust, perhaps the time has come to give ol' Woodsy Owl a serious listening to.

ಬುೊೞ

1978 Charon, a satellite of the dwarf planet Pluto, was discovered. I wonder how small you'd have to be to orbit Pluto. Maybe Charon will turn out to just one of John McEnroe's mis-hit serves from 1977.

1776 The final draft of Declaration of Independence was submitted to the Continental Congress in Philadelphia. With Spell Check still over 200 years away however, the word *unalienable* remained, leaving *inalienable* forever on the outside of history, looking in.

ಬುೊೞ

1860 The Secret Service was formed, though I'm still not sure how we would know that.

1969 Apollo 11 returned to Earth, making Neil Armstrong the first man ever return to Earth after becoming the first man to ever step on the moon. Later that day, he became the first man ever to eat a turkey sandwich after becoming the first man to ever step on the moon. Further, he then became the first … ok, I'll stop now.

৪০৪

1851 The window tax was abolished in Britain, though it did give Connecticut lawmakers an idea for taxation even they hadn't thought of before.

1981 The Supreme Court decided that male-only draft registration was Constitutional, apparently after realizing that all males on the Court involved in making the decision were too old to be drafted.

৪০৪

1876 Custer's Last Stand took place when General George Armstrong Custer took on the Cheyenne and Sioux tribes, and emerged severely unvictorious. What's worse is that not only did he lose the battle, he cost gamblers thousands when he didn't even cover the spread.

1984 Pitcher Vida Blue was suspended for the season due to drug use. He then legally changed his name to Steve Howe, and was immediately credited with seven more chances.

৪০৪

1835 The first sugar cane plantation was started in Hawaii. When informed of the milestone, an aide to the governor responded, "sweet."

৪০৪

1940 Turkey declared its neutrality in World War II, catching Franklin Roosevelt somewhat by surprise. After hearing the news, he told a nearby reporter that he wasn't even aware domestic poultry could talk.

1985   Route 66 ceased to be an official U.S. highway, leaving distraught Americans with virtually no place left to get their kicks.

୫୨Cଔ

1846   New York and Boston were linked by telegraph wires. A Bronx telegraph office received the first message which read, of course, *Yankees suck!*

767   St. Paul I ended his reign as the Catholic Pope. He then signed a multiyear contract to lead the Episcopalians through the 772 season.

୫୨Cଔ

1967   Beatle George Harrison was fined £6 for speeding. I don't know exactly where he was ticketed, but for what amounts to a $10 fine, I can guarantee you it wasn't in Connecticut.

1850   Coal was discovered on Vancouver Island, finally giving credence to Santa Claus's long and publicly stated belief that the kids on that island constantly misbehaved.

୫୨Cଔ

1854   The Netherlands decided to allow corporal punishment. Lieutenants, captains and majors, however, could still do whatever they damn well pleased without fear of repercussions.

1859   Charles Blondin became the first man to cross the Niagara Falls gorge on a tightrope. Blondin later told the press it just goes to show that, at times, there really is only a thin line between life and death.

❧☙

1934   The Portsmouth (Ohio) Spartans of the National Football League became the Detroit Lions. The Lions are currently on pace to match the Spartans win total in December 2044.

JULY _____ 1

1867   Canada became a self-governing dominion of Great Britain. Having learned its lesson the hard way, Britain wisely left the Canadian tea completely untaxed.

❧☙

1943   The first tax withholding to come directly from workers paychecks took place. Over the years, this has somehow evolved into withholding a little pay for you directly from your tax check.

1776   At Independence Hall in Philadelphia, Pennsylvania, the Second Continental Congress voted to approve Virginia's motion for a Declaration of Independence. The tie breaking vote was texted in by a kid from New Hampshire who'd thought he was voting for the American Idol winner.

❧☙

1843   During a thunderstorm in South Carolina an alligator fell from sky. The gator got back on his feet, looked up at the gawkers and said, "What can I tell you? They were all out of cats and dogs."

1971   Singer Jim Morrison died in Paris, France, thus closing The Doors on a promising career.

෨෬

1984   The Dolphin rocket was launched off southern California's San Clemente Island, which explains why Flipper was called faster than lightning.

1939   The New York Yankees retired Lou Gehrig's # 4, making it Major League Baseball's first retired number. They bought the four a Buick and a golf cart, and sent them to down to Naples, Florida.

෨෬

1970   American Top 40 debuted on Los Angeles radio with its host, Casey Kasem. This caused a nationwide panic for kids everywhere who worried he'd give up chasing ghosts with Scooby Doo.

෨෬

1826   The second and third U.S. presidents, John Adams and Thomas Jefferson, both of whom were responsible for writing our Declaration of Independence, passed away on this same day. Exactly 50 years to the day their Declaration was adopted by Congress. No joke, just an unbelievable coincidence.

Independence Day Quotes, the *Spirit of '76*

"I know not what course others may take; but as for me, give me liberty or give me death."

—Patrick Henry to the Virginia House of Burgesses (1775)

"To arms, the regulars are out tonight, the regulars are out!"

—Boston silversmith Paul Revere riding horseback through Lexington, Massachusetts (April 18–19, 1775)

"Resolved: That these united colonies are, and of right ought to be, free and independent states; that they are absolved from all allegiance to the British crown, and that all political connection between them and the state of Great Britain is—and ought to be—totally dissolved."

—Richard Henry Lee, in a proposal to the Second Continental Congress at Independence Hall in Philadelphia, Pennsylvania (June 7, 1776)

"If we don't hang together, we most assuredly will hang separately."

—Benjamin Franklin, joking about the potential fate of the Continental Congress (1776)

"So King George in London may read it without his spectacles."

—John Hancock, president of the Second Continental Congress, in response to the question as to why he made his signature so large on the Declaration of Independence (July 4, 1776)

"I only regret that I have but one life to lose for my country."

—Connecticut schoolteacher and colonial spy Nathan Hale on a British scaffold prior to being hung (September 22, 1776)

"My God, it's all over."

—Britain's Lord North, after hearing the news that General Charles Cornwallis surrendered to General George Washington at Yorktown, Virginia, in October 1781

" ... We hold these truths to be self-evident, that all men are created equal. That they are endowed by their Creator with certain unalienable rights; that among these are Life, Liberty and the Pursuit of Happiness ... and for support of this Declaration, with a firm reliance on the protection of divine Providence, we mutually pledge to each other our lives, our fortunes, and our sacred honor."

—Thomas Jefferson (Excerpted from the Declaration of Independence, 1776)

1610   John Guy set sail from Newfoundland, which up until that point had been known as Notquitefoundland.

❧ ❧

1865   England enacted the world's first maximum speed law, though with the cap set at 5 MPH, there evidently wasn't much difference between the right, left and center lanes.

1946   Former president George W. Bush and actor Sylvester Stallone were born. Oddly, one made a career of being serious, though he'd rather intentionally be funny; and the other would rather come off as serious, but often managed to be unintentionally funny.

❧ ❧

1957   Teenagers Paul McCartney and John Lennon met at a church function in England. They accidentally bumped into each other, knocking Lennon's chocolate into McCartney's peanut butter. The rest, of course, was history.

Also on this date: (1944)—The worst circus fire in American history took place at the Ringling Bros., Barnum & Bailey show in Hartford, Connecticut. If your Hartford roots go back far enough, your family most likely has a story about this tragedy. This is my memoriam to those lost on Barbour Street that day.

1928 In Missouri, the Chillicothe Baking Company became the first one ever to sell sliced bread. At a press conference to announce it, a spokesman told reporters, "This is the greatest thing since … since … Oh, man. Sorry—I got nothing."

ഇ⊙രു

1998 Major League Baseball held its 69th All-Star classic at Coors Field in Denver, Colorado, an event that elevated the game to new heights.

1835 Once again, the Liberty Bell fractured. Proving—and not for the first time—that it was all that it was cracked up to be.

ഇ⊙രു

1994 A Preliminary trial ruling revealed that there was enough evidence to try O.J. Simpson, though evidently there ultimately was too much evidence to convict him.

ഇ⊙രു

1990 At one point on this day, the time and date were 12:34:56 7/8/90. The very next second it was 12:34:57 7/8/90, though to much less fanfare.

1893   Dr. Daniel Williams completed the first successful open heart surgery performed without anesthesia. When the patient was asked after by reporters how he felt, he momentarily paused his bloodcurdling screams to shout, "Who the hell's bright idea was this?!"

ಶಃ

1872   Maine sea captain John Blondel patented the doughnut cutter, which henceforth allowed him to run rings around the competition.

ಶಃ

1955   The song *Rock Around the Clock* by Bill Haley and His Comets reached the top of the Billboard chart. Unfortunately, Haley had overlooked that in 1955, radio stations did not broadcast 24 hours a day.

1865   Mary Surratt, for her part in the Lincoln conspiracy, became the first female executed in the United States. If she'd been sentenced to death in Connecticut, she would still be alive to this day.

ಶಃ

1040   Lady Godiva rode naked on horseback in an effort to get her husband, the Earl of Mercia, to lower taxes in the town of Coventry. So, was that 1040A.D., or 1040EZ?

☞   *Born on this date: Beatrice Mickiewicz—Wonderful American great-grandmother (1904)*   ☜

1673   The Netherlands and Denmark signed a defense treaty. Denmark took no chances, even going so far as to hire Tom Landry.

৩০০৩

1924   Canada signed a trade agreement with the Netherlands; and finally, at long last, they were able to obtain quality Dutch cocoa to go with their poutine.

1979   The Island of Kiribati declared independence from Great Britain. Evidently, it was just their turn.

৩০০৩

1957   Leroy Burney became the first U.S. Surgeon General to connect smoking with lung cancer. Not satisfied to stop there, Burney then went on to connect water consumption with quenching thirst and oxygen intake with breathing.

1832   Henry Schoolcraft discovered the source of the Mississippi River. It turned out to be a water faucet in Minnesota that was left on intentionally by Mark Twain, in an attempt to combat writer's block.

৩০০৩

1898   Radio was patented Guglielmo Marconi, after he got tired of trying to find longer and longer lengths of string to connect his two soup cans with.

1999   Major League Baseball's umpires voted to resign and not finish out the season's final month. No one noticed until players and fans started wondering why the quality of the calls had gone up.

&CB

1990   In Canada, Edward "Fast Eddy" McDonald did a record 8,437 loops with his yo-yo in one hour. After his performance, he discovered he'd significantly overestimated the number of female groupies he'd expected to attend.

1979   President Jimmy Carter gave his famous "Malaise" speech, where he characterized the greatest threat to the country as "this crisis in the growing doubt about the meaning of our own lives and in the loss of a unity of purpose for our nation," thus removing all doubt that Carter was a "glass half empty" kind of guy.

&CB

1870   Georgia was the last Confederate state readmitted to the Union. They were admonished by Mississippi though to either wipe their feet on the matt, or leave their shoes at the door.

&CB

1876   The first no-hitter in baseball history was thrown against the Hartford Dark Blues. Only Hartford could be involved in pro sports for 10 seconds and set a record for futility. It wouldn't surprise me at all to discover that pitching against us for St. Louis that day was Patrick Roy.

1969   Apollo 11 Astronauts Neil Armstrong, Edwin "Buzz" Aldrin and Michael Collins blasted off for their historic moon landing. Unfortunately, they'd already broken through the Earth's atmosphere when Collins realized he'd left the iron on.

ଚ୬

1935   Parking meters were installed for the first time in Oklahoma City, where they've been nickel and diming us to death ever since.

ଚ୬

1251   According to legend, Simon Stork was given a haircut by The Virgin Mary. I can only imagine Stork sitting there in the chair, frantically trying to determine the consequences of under tipping.

1955   Disneyland opened in Anaheim, California, proving the old adage true that one can indeed build a better Mousetrap.

ଚ୬

1473   Charles the Stout conquered Nijmegen. Evidently, the 15th century wasn't all that big on political correctness.

1932   The U.S. and Canada signed a treaty to develop the St. Lawrence Seaway. The treaty ultimately broke down though when neither country wanted to plug the hose in on its own side.

ଚ୬

1872   Secret ballot voting was introduced in Britain. Not to be outdone, some democratic precincts across the pond introduced multiple ballot voting, though in secret.

ഇരുജ

1994   The Crayola Company announced the introduction of scented crayons into the marketplace. Left unannounced was that they'd all produce the same scent—wax.

1978   In the Yukon, the United States and Canada began a 10 year program to rebuild Alaskan highways. I guess we'll just have to take their word for it.

ഇരുജ

1990   Richard Nixon's presidential library opened in California. Reports were that the literary wing was fine, but the library's audio wing left something to be desired.

1969   Apollo 11 astronauts Neil Armstrong and Edwin "Buzz" Aldrin landed on the moon. A dejected Aldrin later lamented that if only they could've anticipated eBay, they would've grabbed a lot more rocks.

ഇരുജ

1994   O.J. Simpson offered a half million dollar reward for any evidence leading to the identity of Nicole Brown's killer. After careful consideration however, he decided it would be bad form if he simply went ahead and collected it from himself.

ഇരുജ

1976 NASA's Viking 1 spacecraft landed on Mars, where just as they'd suspected, they'd found only men.

1969 Neil Armstrong became the first human being to walk on the Moon, an act that immediately condemned thousands of male Generation Xers to the name Neil.

৪০৫৪

1904 The first grain elevator in Montreal, Quebec was completed. Unfortunately the grain, being inanimate, had no way to push the buttons.

☞ *Born on this date: Christopher J. Gay (1972—Hartford, Connecticut)—American writer and voice-over artist. C'mon now, you know very well that I couldn't just leave myself out of my own book.* ☜

1587 A second English colony, also fated to vanish under mysterious circumstances, was established on Roanoke Island. Said the third group of potential colonists prior to leaving England, "Screw this; we're staying right here."

৪০৫৪

1975 Confederate General Robert E. Lee's United States citizenship was restored by the House of Representatives. By all accounts, Lee took the news lying down.

1764 Massachusetts Revolutionary lawyer and political orator James Otis published his opinion on taxation without representation, writing: *Not a fan, England. LOL.*

৪০৩

1886 New York bookmaker Steve Brodie *allegedly* survived a jump off the Brooklyn Bridge. Please understand that I'm no doctor, but my thought is that this should not have been all that difficult to verify.

1959 Vice President Richard Nixon argued with Soviet Premier Nikita Khrushchev during their "Kitchen Debate." The argument started when, while preparing a special meal for both of them, Nixon tried breaking the ice with the awful pun *I've got no thyme for this.*

৪০৩

2005 Cyclist Lance Armstrong retired after winning his record setting seventh consecutive Tour de France. His fans were relieved however when it eventually became clear that Armstrong's departure in fact turned out to only be a *Brett Favre* retirement.

1868 Congress created the Wyoming Territory, citing America's pressing need for a suitable place to hold rodeos.

৪০৩

1962 The House passed a bill requiring equal pay for equal work—regardless of sex. Upon being made aware of the ruling, workers representing both genders simultaneously told the House, "Ok then, we might as well take sex, too."

1981 New York Mayor Ed Koch was given the Heimlich maneuver while eating in a Chinese restaurant. About an hour later, he requested it again.

꿍

1874   Alexander Graham Bell described to his father his idea for the telephone, though some people felt that Bell was just trying to open a line up a line of communication with him.

1959   William Shea announced his plan to bring a baseball team back to New York City in 1961. Unfortunately, those plans fell through when all he was able to acquire were the Mets.

꿍

1789   The Department of Foreign Affairs was established by Congress. The action drew criticism from world leaders en masse, who felt that any extramarital dalliances in their collective countries were, quite frankly, none of our business.

☞ *Lost on this date: My beautiful little sister, Chelsea Marie (June 30, 1987–July 27, 2002) You're always in my heart, Chels …* 🖜

1586   The first potato arrived in Britain. It took hours to get to the hotel, though, due to the seemingly endless swarms of paparazzi.

꿍

1540   England's King Henry VIII executed Thomas Cromwell, and then later that day married his fifth wife, Catherine Howard. It appears that Hank was also the king of multitasking.

1981   Britain's Prince Charles married Lady Diana Spencer at St. Paul's Cathedral in London. I think—if memory serves—that might have even been televised.

ഔരു

1874   A portable tennis court was patented by Walter Wingfield. For some reason, he'd had an incredible urge to call it Pong.

1966   England won soccer's World Cup. No official fan casualty figures exist, however.

ഔരു

1983   Andy Bean sank a two-inch putt with his club handle, resulting in a two-stroke penalty that cost him the Canadian Open—by two strokes. This appears to be one guy who literally needed to get a grip.

1774   Oxygen was discovered by Joseph Priestley. Fortunately for Priestly, his lungs had already made that same discovery decades earlier.

ഔരു

1997   The Oakland Athletics traded Mark McGwire to the St. Louis Cardinals, who ultimately ended up getting more than what they had initially "bargained" for.

AUGUST

1981   MTV debuted with The Buggles's *Video Killed The Radio Star.* Remembering this factoid is important, as it may very well be the only evidence MTV ever aired music videos.

ഇരു

1994   Pope John Paul received a record breaking $8.75 Million advance for his book, titled *Crossing the Threshold of Hope,* with the sequel tentatively titled the slightly more egregious *Crossing the Threshold of Bank of America.*

1776   Delegates to the Second Continental Congress began signing our Declaration of Independence. They thought momentarily about celebrating forevermore on this date but then realized that they'd already ordered the stationery bearing *July 4.*

ഇരു

1876   "Wild Bill" Hickok was killed by gunfire while playing poker at a saloon in South Dakota. As he lay dying, he told the bartender that it would be the last time he'd ever order a shot in this place.

1970   England's Miriam Hargrave passed her driving test on her 40th try. Well, I guess that just proves the old adage true: *If at first you don't succeed, try try again, 39 more times.*

ഇരു

1914   Germany declared war on France. You know, I could swear I've done this one before.

ଛଡ଼

881   At the Battle at Saucourt, French King Louis III beat the Vikings. In fairness to the Vikings though, they had rested Brett Favre for the playoffs.

1693   Dom Perignon invented Champagne. He followed it up a week later with an invention he referred to as *aspirin.*

ଛଡ଼

1837   Traveling alone, Thomas Simpson reached Barrow Point, Alaska and then took possession of it for Britain. However, it was only after he fended off a pack of vampires who were there for 30 days of night.

ଛଡ଼

1983   New York Yankee outfielder Dave Winfield accidentally killed a seagull with a thrown ball. In fairness to Winfield, the bird had tried to take third base on him.

1926   Harry Houdini stayed in a coffin underwater for an hour and a half. Afterward, he said he would've come up sooner but he'd been practically dead tired.

ଛଡ଼

2000   Actor Alec Guinness passed away at age 86, as apparently The Force was no longer with him.

1964   The world's oldest tree was cut down after achieving the age of 4,900. When asked in an interview later why he did it, the saw wielding perpetrator answered, "I don't know. It just seemed like the cruel thing to do."

಄಄

1995   Both the Indians and Browns played in Cleveland on same day for the first time ever and, not surprisingly, both lost. Maybe they should've played each other.

1956   The Red Sox fined Ted Williams $5,000 for spitting at Boston fans, literally forcing Williams to put his money where his mouth was.

಄಄

1820   The first potatoes were planted in Hawaii. In retribution, Idaho and Maine planted two thousand acres each of macadamia nuts.

1911   The one millionth patent was filed with the U.S. Patent Office. Ironically, the patent was for a large net used to hold, and then release, thousands of balloons.

಄಄

1931   Hoover Dam workers went on strike. It wasn't long, however, before those dam workers went back to their dam work.

1892   Thomas Edison received a patent for his Two Way Telegraph, after realizing the original version of his invention, the One Way Telegraph, made for a very boring conversation.

ॐ

1995   Grateful Dead singer Jerry Garcia passed away from a heart attack at age 53. Shortly thereafter, Ben and Jerry's decided the best way to honor the man was to name a high fat, calorie laden ice cream after him.

1821   Missouri became the 24th state, with the stipulation that residents would not be allowed to pronounce the "i" at the end of its name.

ॐ

1776   Word of the United States Declaration of Independence reached London. A short time later, the photo of a furious, scepter wielding King George III appeared on the back page of a New York paper under the caption, "Oh, it is SO on!"

1896   Harvey Hubbell patented the electric light bulb socket with a pull chain. He remarked later that he was holding a light bulb over his head trying to figure out the best way install it, when he was suddenly struck with a good idea.

ॐ

1874   Harry Parmelee patented the sprinkler head. He told reporters afterward that he persevered, even while most of his friends kept telling him his idea was all wet.

1960   Echo I, the first communications satellite, was launched. Unfortunately all that scientists on Earth received from it was the same information repeated back to them, over and over again.

ഔഽ

1856   Anthony Fass patented the accordion and unwittingly forever changed the course of Weird Al Yankovic's life.

1960   The first two way telephone conversation by satellite took place. It lasted only 30 seconds though, as the caller realized he did not have the $4,000 in dimes needed to continue it for the next three minutes.

ഔഽ

1917   The Phillies stole five bases in one inning against Boston. I hadn't realized Jason Varitek had played for Boston that long.

1979   A rainbow was visible for three hours in Northern Wales. It unintentionally lead directly to the capture of over 1,300 leprechauns.

ഔഽ

1893   France introduced motor vehicle registration, though, more than a century later, they still haven't been able replicate the eternal wait at the DMV that we have perfected here in the United States.

1965   The Beatles played in front of over 60,000 fans in Queens, New York, something the Mets are still hoping to do someday.

ଫୋୠ

1939   The Wizard of Oz premiered in Hollywood. One movie critic wrote, "Though I liked the movie overall, for a good majority it just seemed to lack courage, brains, and heart."

1948 and 1977 respectively   Babe Ruth and Elvis Presley passed away. In both instances, flags at McDonald's were flown at half mast.

ଫୋୠ

1861   President Abraham Lincoln prohibited the Union from trading with Confederacy, consequently forcing the Union to finish out the 1861 season without the left-handed middle reliever they so desperately needed.

ଫୋୠ

1959   Oil was first discovered in the Yukon. In an unrelated story, also on this date preliminary plans for a war in the Yukon were first discussed.

ଫୋୠ

1896 Prospectors found gold in Alaska, touching off another Gold Rush. This one never got the same coverage as the previous one in San Francisco, however, as the "Klondike '96ers" just didn't have the same ring to it.

1914 President Woodrow Wilson issued his *Proclamation of Neutrality,* which was designed to keep the U.S. out of World War I. So it would seem that all those American soldiers were merely vacationing in Europe, simultaneously.

୫୦ଓଃ

1988 George H.W. Bush nominated Indiana Senator Dan Quayle as his running mate during the Republican National Convention in New Orleans, proving once and for all that Republicans do indeed have a sense of humor.

1951 St. Louis owner Bill Veeck sent 3' 7" Eddie Gaedel up to pinch-hit, for what ended up being a very short at bat.

୫୦ଓଃ

1934 Ohio hosted the first All-American Soap Box Derby, leaving many reporters in the mainstream media with nothing to stand on for the entire day.

1998 Canada's Supreme Court ruled that Quebec cannot legally secede without the federal government's approval. Well, duh; but if you need permission to secede, then what's the point?

୫୦ଓଃ

1920   Detroit's WWJ became the first commercial radio station to begin operations. They soon folded though, after discovering an "all commercials" format wasn't as appealing to the public as they thought it might be.

1841   The Venetian Blind was first patented in United States. I'll now pause for a moment so you can all commit that to memory.

ಬಿ೦ಿ

1858   The famed Abraham Lincoln–Stephen Douglas debates began. Being August 21 however, and with nothing else going on, they debated the usefulness of the Venetian blind.

1911   Vincenzo Peruggia stole the Mona Lisa. He simply walked right past the guard station and out of the Louvre with it. I have no proof of course, but I can only assume that this was the first recorded use on Earth of the Jedi Mind Trick.

ಬಿ೦ಿ

1973   Richard Nixon named Henry Kissinger Secretary of State, after discovering Kissinger could type over 90 words a minute.

1566   The Netherlands granted rights to Calvinists, while the Hobbesists, sadly, got nothing.

ಬಿ೦ಿ

1904 The automobile tire chain was patented. It was a little premature however, as snow wasn't patented until 1907.

2006 The International Astrological Union redefined the term "planet" to the extent that Pluto was no longer considered one. Asked for a comment on the IAU's decision after the ruling, Pluto responded, "Sure. Screw them."

৪০৫৪

1853 In upstate New York, Chef George Crum invented potato chips. What were the chances? That'd be akin to the paper towel being invented by Suzie Spillsalot.

1921 The United States signed a peace treaty with Germany, who had evidently used invisible ink.

৪০৫৪

1830 The Belgian Revolution began. It didn't last long however, as combatants quickly realized that waffles had had little effect on each other, no matter how hard they threw them.

580 Toilet paper was invented in China, proving that at least one ancient civilization gave a crap about their citizens' comfort.

৪০৫৪

1929 The first roller coaster in the United States was built, though only after the project went through several ups and downs.

1984 President Reagan informed the public of the Teacher in Space project, which was quickly endorsed unanimously by every single grade school kid in America.

ഇന്റ

1990 A game between Milwaukee and Toronto was delayed over a half hour due to swarm of gnats. More than a few New York Yankee players pointed out that gnats the way they do things in Cleveland, too.

1898 North Carolina pharmacist Caleb Bradham rechristened his carbonated beverage *Brad's Drink* as *Pepsi-Cola*. Bradham explained that he discovered Pepsi-Cola was an old Native American term meaning *cash cow.*

ഇന്റ

1938 Northwestern University gave an honorary degree to Charlie McCarthy. Does it strike anyone else as odd that this esteemed educational institution had no perception issues with literally giving one of their degrees to a dummy?

ഇന്റ

1964 The Beatles met Bob Dylan, though they couldn't decipher whatever hell he was trying to say, either.

1919 In Canada, after several years of no cars, Prince Edward Island removed its ban on automobiles. The decision was made after local politicians realized that without cars, they couldn't issue parking tickets.

ᑭᏋᏏ

1896   In New York City, chop suey was first created. Ironically, it was the same day that hot dogs and apple pie were invented
in Beijing.

1146   With the intention of ending war forever, European leaders outlawed crossbows. Indeed, were every conventional weapon
worldwide to disappear tomorrow, within a week some guy would
undoubtedly devise a slingshot out of sugarcane with the capac-
ity to propel marshmallows at the speed of sound.

ᑭᏋᏏ

1963   A hotline was established between American and Soviet
leaders. For the first week that the bright red phone was hooked
up however, neither Kennedy nor Khrushchev could resist making crank calls to each other.

ᑭᏋᏏ

1797   *Frankenstein* author Mary Shelley was born in London,
England. The rest of her biography is available elsewhere, in bits
and pieces.

1935   President Franklin Roosevelt signed an act which prevented the export of U.S. arms to belligerents. Surely it was FDR's
ability to make tough decisions like these that got him elected
four times.

ᑭᏋᏏ

1955   The first sun-powered car was demonstrated in Chicago, after they'd tried unsuccessfully for a week to get it to work in Seattle.

1752   The Liberty Bell arrived in Philadelphia. It had been ordered from Whitechapel Foundry who, evidently, employed a crack team of bell casters.

ഇരുൽ

1939   Switzerland proclaimed its neutrality in World War II. When asked to explain their reasoning to the world press, one Swiss official answered, "I guess you could say that we don't really feel that strongly about it, one way or the other."

1992   The United States and Russia agreed to build a space station. Both were equally disappointed however, when it was discovered that their unanimous choice for its name, *The Death Star,* had already been trademarked by some guy named Lucas.

ഇരുൽ

1797   In Quebec, Canada, Catholic bishops were required to swear an oath of allegiance to the British Crown. This, of course, created the rare phenomenon of integration between church and state.

ഇരുൽ

1651   In Canada, Martin Boutet was named first town crier of Quebec. The job didn't pay much, but it did come with a lifetime supply of Ricola.

1894   Labor Day was celebrated in Canada for the first time. Finally at long last much needed relief was brought to the millions of expectant Canadian mothers who'd been stuck in perpetual gestational limbo.

ဆာၣ

1752   England adopted the Gregorian calendar, effectively wiping away this day and ten that followed. This caused riots within the British populace who'd thought the government stole time away from their lives. You know I can relate, as I felt the same way that time I turned on C-Span.

1957   Ford began selling the Edsel, the designer of which then went on to create Yugos and Betamax, and head up the Michael Dukakis presidential campaign.

ဆာၣ

1866   The first Hawaiian daily newspaper was published. It was called the *Daily Who Cares What Goes On Elsewhere People; You Live In Hawaii.*

1698   Russian Tsar Peter I imposed a tax on beards. When questioned by the press as to where he came up with such an outrageous idea, he responded that he used to be a lawmaker in Connecticut.

ဆာၣ

1885   The first gasoline pump was delivered to a dealer in Indiana, who then set an industry precedent by turning around and hosing the rest of us with it.

ৰ০অ৪

1839   The First Opium War began in China, though after only a short while it was all good, man.

1977   The Canadian Wheat Board sold Viet Nam 120,000 metric tons of wheat. However, surviving footage of the transaction turned out to be somewhat grainy.

ৰ০অ৪

1964   President Lyndon Johnson gave British Columbia Premier W.A.C. Bennett a $273,291,661.25 check as payment for the Columbia River Power agreement. I don't know what I would've liked to have watched more—Johnson sitting there trying to write that amount out on the legal line, or Bennett going up to the teller with the check to cash it.

1251 B.C.   The legendary Hercules was born. I guess now you could say he was strong, and not forgotten.

ৰ০অ৪

1986   Cleveland became the NFL's first team to have a play reviewed through instant replay. The technology was scuttled though when a consensus of fans agreed no one wanted to have to see any Browns plays more than once.

1966   Star Trek premiered on NBC, beginning its three-year mission to boldly go where few shows had gone before—lucrative syndication.

೮ഠരു

1995   The Cleveland Indians clinched the American League's Central Division title. I'm just putting that sentence in writing here, as you may never see it again, unless some Hollywood producer decides to make *Major League 4.*

1992   The Baltimore Orioles drew three million fans for the first time in their history. That is truly a remarkable stat, as I wouldn't have thought the O's could've ever drawn that many people, short of using a sketch artist.

೮ഠരു

1926   The Radio Corporation of America (RCA) created the National Broadcasting Company, (NBC) who opened up with a Thursday night lineup of what they termed *Must Hear Radio.*

೮ഠരು

1776   The Continental Congress officially changed our name from the United Colonies to the United States of America. Sentences like that always give me pause. They allow me to temporarily overlook the constant, unending vitriol spewed back and forth between partisan Democrats and Republicans, and reflect on this great country of ours—and what it took to make it so.

1776   Coventry, Connecticut schoolteacher Nathan Hale volunteered to spy for General George Washington. As a spy, he turned out to be a good schoolteacher with a penchant for getting off spectacular one-liners.

ॐ⋈

1894   English taxi driver George Smith became the first person fined for drunk driving. Well, that didn't take long.

1962   Ringo Starr replaced Pete Best as the Beatles drummer. So, do you still not think timing is everything?

ॐ⋈

1789   Alexander Hamilton was appointed our first Secretary of the Treasury and hence became the first person ever referred to as the Money Man.

ॐ⋈

2001   Arguably the worst tragedy in American history occurred. In honor of our countrymen and women lost that horrific day, I'd like to offer a selection of quotes that came to mind when I first wrote this for my radio broadcast. It is my fervent hope that none of us ever see another such day.

"Those who would sacrifice liberty for a little temporary safety, deserve neither liberty nor safety"

—Benjamin Franklin

"Political correctness is tyranny with manners."

—Charlton Heston

" Oh, say does that Star Spangled Banner, yet wave o'er the land of the free, and the home, of the brave."

—Francis Scott Key

1940 Cave paintings were discovered in France. The paintings were primitive to the extent that one archeologist was prompted to state that they appeared so easy to draw, even a caveman could have done it.

∞🙷

1946 Tide laundry detergent was introduced to the public. It then quickly went out and cleaned up against all competition.

1965 The Beatles released their future classic, *Yesterday*. Regrettably, it was put out one day too late.

∞🙷

1985 Nintendo released Super Mario Bros., though only after they were forced to pay Mario millions to lure him away from his cushy job as second banana to Donkey Kong.

1956 The first prefrontal lobotomy was performed in Washington, D.C. After two weeks of recuperation, however, the congressman returned to work.

∞🙷

1716 America's first lighthouse was lit in Boston Harbor. In that particular instance, it was *one if by sea.*

1982 The first issue of the national newspaper *USA Today* was published. Also on this date: the first person to have no choice but use the awkward phrase, "I saw that in USA Today ... today," used it.

શ્જી

1928 Alexander Fleming discovered penicillin. Although it was a nerve-racking journey to perfect his discovery, it ironically allowed others to breathe easier.

1977 Ringo Starr released his song, *Drowning In the Sea of Love.* He followed it up six months later with, *Rescued By the Reality of Alimony.*

શ્જી

1990 Sam Ackerman, at the age of 101, married his 95 year old bride Eva. Evidently it was the same old story.

1176 The Battle of Myriokephalon was fought. The fight dragged on for days, with occasional pauses so that somebody or other could buy a vowel.

શ્જી

1953 The first successful separation of Siamese twins took place. Shortly thereafter however, both twins expressed sadness at feeling what they'd described as a sudden disconnect between them.

1679   New Hampshire became a county of the Massachusetts Bay Colony, prompting New Hampshire's governor to state, "Well, this isn't going to do much for our self esteem."

80C3

1977   Voyager 1 took the first photograph of the Earth and Moon together, thus leaving the moon with a lot of explaining to do to its wife.

1959   Soviet leader Nikita Khrushchev was barred from visiting Disneyland. It was nothing political, he was told; it was just that he wasn't tall enough to ride the rides.

80C3

1849   In California, the first commercial laundry was established. It was a dirty job—but somebody had to do it.

1951   The first North Pole jet crossing took place. A potential tragedy was averted at the last second when the pilot was able to steer clear of a wayward Comet and Blitzen.

80C3

1976   Playboy released Jimmy Carter's interview where he admitted that he lusted for women. The shocking revelation relegated Carter, in the minds of a stunned American public, to the ranks of a small group that contained virtually every other man on the face of the Earth.

1958   The first airplane flight to exceed 12 hours landed in Dallas, Texas. Not as widely mentioned was that it had originated from Fort Worth.

ଽୠେଷ

1966   Five inches of rain cascaded down on New York City, thus giving a whole new meaning to the term "waterfall."

1776   Nathan Hale was hanged for spying during American Revolution. His last words were, "I only regret that I have but one life to lose for my country." He then fictitiously added, "And you can quote me on that."

ଽୠେଷ

1921   Lithuania and Estonia were admitted to the League of Nations. They were required to pay a 50 million dollar expansion fee, but in return were allowed to pick first and second overall in the 1922 League of Nations Entry Draft.

1806   The Lewis and Clark expedition returned to St. Louis from the Pacific Northwest, where they subsequently proclaimed to President Thomas Jefferson that he was now free to move about the country.

ଽୠେଷ

1986   Congress selected the rose as our national flower. How ironic they chose the flower that, if you don't pay enough attention while dealing with it, can really stick it to you.

1838 The Anti-Corn-Law League was formed in an attempt to repeal the English Corn Law. In fact, the ACLL was so relentless in their quest to have it rescinded that they at one point were accused of "stalking" the corn.

જ૦૭

1901 A telegraph connection was completed between Yukon and southern Canada. Evidently this was accomplished to allow southern Canada to finally be able to communicate with its polar bears.

303 While on a voyage in Amiens, France, Saint Fermin of Pamplona was beheaded. Later that night in his journal he wrote, *That settles it—I'm never coming here again.*

જ૦૭

1911 Ground was broken for Fenway Park in Boston. This was just days after the design plan for Fenway's outfield dimensions were submitted by Pablo Picasso.

જ૦૭

1804 The Teton Sioux demanded a boat from Lewis and Clark as a toll for moving upriver, thus giving Clark the preliminary idea for the New Jersey Turnpike.

1777   During the American Revolution, British troops occupied Philadelphia, Pennsylvania. Years later, after having lost the war, British General Howe admitted the outcome was most likely due to them never having stayed in a Holiday Inn Express.

ନ୍ଦୁଓଷ

1890   The U.S. stopped minting the three-cent piece, leaving Americans with no other choice but to start putting their two cents in going forward whenever they had an opinion.

1777   Lancaster, Pennsylvania, was the capital of the United States for one day, after winning the grand prize on Fox's prime time game show, *Who Wants To Be The Capital Of The United States For One Day?*

ନ୍ଦୁଓଷ

1892   The Diamond Match Company patented the matchbook, which immediately caught fire with the public.

1996   Baltimore Oriole Roberto Alomar was suspended five games for spitting at an umpire. The suspension was levied after Alomar's excuse—that he was merely voluntarily submitting a saliva sample as part of a random drug test—proved to be simply implausible.

ନ୍ଦୁଓଷ

1944   The Battle of Arnhem took place, as Mickey Mouse squared off against Goofy, and Donald Duck took on Cinderella. Oh, wait—sorry. That was the Battle of Anaheim.

1829   London's reorganized police force, which later became known as Scotland Yard, went on duty. When asked why that name was chosen, a police leftenant explained to the press that it was because the domain name "englandyard.com" had already been taken.

೮ಲ

1987   The television show *thirtysomething* debuted. ABC's drama ultimately proved to be so popular that it produced two successful spin-offs: *sixtysomething* and *deadsomething*.

1659   Peter Stuyvesant forbade tennis playing during religious services. On its surface, this seems like it would've been the least necessary decree, like, ever.

೮ಲ

1888   Jack the Ripper claimed his third and fourth victims in Whitechapel, England. In a testament to the American educational system, someone seriously once asked me my opinion as to why, since he was also enjoying huge popularity in England in 1888, Sherlock Holmes didn't ever try to step in and solve the Ripper crimes.

OCTOBER

1795   Belgium was conquered by France, leading to the origin of the famous saying, *To the victors, go the waffles.*

৪০৩

1971 Walt Disney World opened near Orlando, Florida. Though it has become one of the world's top vacation destinations, many still consider it a Mickey Mouse operation.

1968 A British woman gave birth to the first recorded sextuplets in England's history. When asked about the anomaly, she simply responded that it was no big deal; six of one, half dozen of the other.

৪০৩

1925 John Baird performed the first test of a working television system. However, when he turned the set on and saw what was being broadcast, he scrapped the whole idea, went home, and read a book.

1955 Captain Kangaroo debuted on CBS and The Mickey Mouse Club debuted on ABC. In the undercard, Mr. Green Jeans took down Donald Duck with a devastating uppercut for a third round knockout.

৪০৩

1995 Former Buffalo Bills running back O.J. Simpson was found not guilty by a jury of his fans. Uh, peers.

৪০৩

1964 The first Buffalo wings were made at the Anchor Bar in Buffalo, New York. I completely admit that this item's in my book simply because I love Buffalo, and I figure this ought to be enough to get my picture up on that wall with everybody else.

1923   Actor Charlton Heston was born in Evanston, Illinois. His first words were that you'll take his bottle from his cold, dead hands.

&)(&

1957   Leave it to Beaver debuted on CBS. Though it was never quite made clear what it was that was left to Beaver, it almost certainly was not a long and lucrative acting career.

1987   Canada and the U.S. signed the Free Trade Agreement, which was the primary catalyst in finally allowing the Cubs to acquire Andre Dawson from the Montreal Expos.

&)(&

1990   A Cincinnati jury acquitted a local art gallery of obscenity. Their reasoning was that hosting the *Bengals: Their Team History Through Photographs* exhibit was not technically obscene, just awfully hard to look at.

1979   Pope John Paul II became the first pontiff to visit the White House, where he was received by President Jimmy Carter. After reviewing the administration's performance, the Pope apparently lamented that he should have gotten here much, much sooner.

&)(&

1783   Benjamin Hanks patented the self-winding clock. Everything went fine until Daylight Savings Time ended.

2003 California voters recalled Governor Gray Davis and elected actor Arnold Schwarzenegger to replace him. They then sent Davis out to hunt down and terminate Sarah Connor.

෨෬

2001 San Francisco Giant Barry Bonds hit his record 73rd and final home run of the season. Prorated for legitimacy, the actual total is 42.

1945 President Harry S. Truman announced that the secret of the atomic bomb would be shared only with Britain and Canada, and even then it was only because they had pinky sworn to keep it.

෨෬

1856 The Second Opium War began in China. Needless to say, this one was a little more subdued than the First Opium War.

1002 Leif Erikson landed in present-day North America. An excerpt from his journal that day reads, *Columbus Day, my ass.*

෨෬

1635 Rhode Island Founder Roger Williams was banished from the Massachusetts Bay Colony for speaking out against punishments for religious offences. Apparently Massachusetts wasn't always a Blue state.

1971 The famous London Bridge was reassembled in its new American home of Lake Havasu City, Arizona, irreparably cheapening the song.

⟶⟵

1985 Actor–director Orson Welles passed away at age 70. I can't help but think how wicked cool it would be if his last word had been *Rosebud*.

1991 Televangelist Jimmy Swaggart was seen soliciting a prostitute. The spotter must have had great eyesight too, to be able to distinguish the money grubbing whore ... from the prostitute.

⟶⟵

1929 J.C. Penney opened a store in Delaware, making his a nationwide company with outlets in all 48 states. Not to be outdone, Sears immediately went out and bought Alaska and Hawaii.

1915 The Ford Motor Company manufactured its one millionth Model T automobile, while the Model U continued to sit and stew silently in anger.

⟶⟵

1960 Nikita Khrushchev disrupted a U.N. General Assembly session by pounding his desk with a shoe. You've got to hand it to Khrushchev; that guy had a lot of sole.

1792   The cornerstone of the White House was laid during a ceremony in the District of Columbia, thereby setting a precedent for the JFK, LBJ and Clinton years.

୫୦ଓଃ

1986   "Mad Dog" Vachon retired from pro wrestling citing a lack of desire to perform. He then voluntarily surrendered himself to Michael Vick.

1789   George Washington proclaimed the first Thanksgiving Day; he then kicked back with a case of Sam Adams and watched Dallas play at Detroit.

୫୦ଓଃ

1834   In Philadelphia, Pennsylvania, the Whigs and Democrats staged a gun, stone and brick battle for control of a Moyamensing Township election. Both sides agreed beforehand that staging a rock, paper, scissors battle would've come off to onlookers as too "wussy."

1888   The infamous "From Hell" letter sent by Jack the Ripper was received by authorities, who were ultimately able to trace its place of origin back to the waiting room of the Connecticut Department of Motor Vehicles.

୫୦ଓଃ

1938   The District of Columbia formally adopted a design for its flag. The most realistic design yet, it consisted of an elephant and a donkey playing tug of war over a hundred dollar bill.

1793   Marie Antoinette was guillotined, though she later said of the experience that it was nothing to lose your head over; yet on the other hand it was simply to die for.

ଔଓ

1775   Portland, Maine, was burned by the British, evidently after one too many "Lobster-back" jokes.

☞ *Born on this date: Noah Webster (1758, West Hartford, Connecticut—Famed American lexicographer). I wrote an article on Webster once; he was definitely not fond of excess U's." Feel free to honor his memory; but please, for his sake, don't honour it.*

1814   Nine people perished in the London Beer Flood. I'm guessing that if one could choose a way to go out, this would probably be it.

ଔଓ

1978   President Jimmy Carter restored U.S. citizenship to Jefferson Davis, who was the only president of the seceded Confederate States of America. One wonders whose pardon was next had Carter been reelected—Benedict Arnold's?

1767   The Mason–Dixon Line, separating Maryland and Pennsylvania, was finished; it took over four tons of chalk to complete.

ଔଓ

1867 and 1898 The U.S. took possession of Alaska and Puerto Rico, respectively. The latter because we apparently felt the need to balance out the weather.

1982 John DeLorean was arrested for trafficking cocaine, and suddenly it became clear how he got the idea for those doors.

ဆာယ

1980 Steve McPeak rode a unicycle measuring almost 102 feet high, a feat which brought him to the McPeak of his career.

ဆာယ

1781 At Yorktown, Virginia, British General Cornwallis surrendered to General George Washington, effectively ending the American Revolution. No joke here. If you have some extra time, please read about this amazing time period and learn more about the fascinating circumstances that led to the birth of our great country.

1967 Roger Patterson and Robert Gimlin filmed what they claimed was an authentic Bigfoot. They then spent years rebutting skeptics who'd maintained it was a guy in a suit, by insisting it was just that the Sasquatch had had a zipper shaped birthmark.

ဆာယ

1803 The U.S. Senate ratified the Louisiana Purchase. Shouted one senator who hadn't bothered to read what he had voted for beforehand, *$15 million?! What the hell? I thought we were all just ordering out for some jambalaya.*

1879   Thomas Edison invented a workable electric light at his laboratory in Menlo Park, N.J., stating he at long last came up with something that people could imagine hovering over their head whenever they had a good idea.

ಬಿಂಬ

1917   American soldiers first saw action in World War I on the front lines in France, causing confused reporters to ask Woodrow Wilson exactly then what his personal definition of the word "Neutrality" meant.

1969   Paul McCartney denied rumors of his passing. I'm not certain how long his press conference lasted but, had I been there, I would've been inclined to believe him right from its outset.

ಬಿಂಬ

1787   Balloonist Andre-Jacques Garnerin of Paris made the first parachute descent, landing safely from a height of 3,200 feet. Talk about sailing right into history.

1925   Legendary talk show host Johnny Carson was born in Iowa. It was your typical birth, except for the one odd moment when the doctor announced loudly, "now, heeeeeeeeeeeeeeeeeeeeeeeeeere's Johnny!"

ಬಿಂಬ

4004 BC   According to the calculations of Archbishop James Ussher, the creation of the world began. Scientists ultimately proved his theory correct, give or take 4½ billion years.

1931 New York City's George Washington Bridge opened to public traffic, which may very well be the greatest understatement of all time.

ഇൽൻ

1940 The 40-hour work week went into effect in the United States. Too bad they didn't decide to implement this in, say, 1905.

1760 Britain's King George III succeeded his late grandfather, King George II. So, I'm guessing his dad was King George II ½.

ഇൽൻ

1969 Canadian rock group The Guess Who was awarded a Gold Record for their hit single *Laughing,* which then forced them to add *All the Way to the Bank* to the song's title.

1670 Quebec's Louis Gaboury was jailed for eating meat during Lent. If he's still in hell now, image how pissed he was when centuries later the Vatican changed the rules to allow that sort of thing.

ഇൽൻ

1492 The first lead pencil was used. Having nothing practical to employ it for, its inventor then decided to create the SATs.

2005   Harriet Miers withdrew her nomination to the Supreme Court, after it was suddenly realized that being qualified to be on the Supreme Court was one of its primary qualifications.

ଽଔ୰ଔଷ

1947   The radio show *You Bet Your Life* premiered, starring Groucho Marx. Ultimately, Marx lost the bet.

1793   Eli Whitney applied for a patent for his cotton gin, though he soon realized that spun alcohol wrapped around a stick would never catch on as well as cotton candy did.

ଽଔ୰ଔଷ

1741   Fish glue was first made in Quebec, after some heavy lobbying from the Untied Horses Union of Canada.

☞   *Born on this date: Dr. Jonas Salk (1914)—Renowned American scientist. Dr. Salk defeated polio and, as such, prevented much suffering and saved countless lives.*   ☜

1982   The Michael Jackson/Paul McCartney song *The Girl Is Mine* was released. Were I a betting man, my bet would've been that "The Girl" ended up with McCartney.

ଽଔ୰ଔଷ

1945   57 years after it was patented, the first ballpoint pen went on sale. 57 years? Talk about a write of passage. (*Author's Note: Yes, that joke was indeed awful. You know it; I know it. So I'm going to write a third one just to make up for it. Please see below.*)

ॐ○ৎ

1727   A rare but severe earthquake took place here in New England. Seismologists were able to trace it back to David Ortiz trying to run out an infield single.

1938   Orson Welles, after his radio broadcast of H.G. Wells's *The War of the Worlds,* tricked the Nation into believing we were being attacked by Martians. I'm not sure, but my guess is it would be just as easy for him to pull this off today, too.

ॐ○ৎ

1988   Philip Morris purchased Kraft Foods for over $13 billion, after their marketing department decided that they could sell the public on the notion that a good cigarette was the perfect way to top off a piping hot bowl of macaroni and cheese.

☞ *Born on this date: John Adams (1735)—Founding Father, second U.S. president. Like his predecessor George Washington, Adams had integrity and was an extremely honest politician. I wonder if it was fate, or simply luck of the draw, that we used most of them up at the country's outset.* ☜

1978   Michael Myers returned to the sleepy Midwestern town of Haddonfield, Illinois, to wreak havoc on an unsuspecting ... Oh, sorry; it's Halloween and I'm not really paying attention. Trick or Treat.

&Cß

1926 Magician Harry Houdini found a way to escape old age by passing away from a ruptured appendix.

&Cß

834 All Hallows Eve was observed for the first time to honor the saints—Roger Moore and Val Kilmer.

NOVEMBER _____

1928 The first celebration of Author's Day took place. It turned out to be something to really write home about.

&Cß

1992 Montreal's McGill University was named the best in Canada, narrowly edging out ... Well, I'm sure another very good school.

_____

1959 Charles Van Doren admitted to a House subcommittee that he'd received the questions and answers in advance of his appearances on the TV game show *Twenty-One*. He also added that after careful consideration, he'd determined it was a lot easier to win that way.

&Cß

1961 Singer k.d. lang was born in Canada, evidently prior to the advent of capital letters.

1752   Georg Friedrich Handel underwent an unsuccessful eye operation. That's a tough break. It's hard to imagine that an 18th century optical procedure wouldn't have worked out for the best.

❧☙

1955   An Alabama woman was bruised by a meteor. I'm not certain what's more remarkable, that she was struck by a meteor, or that she was struck by a meteor, yet only bruised. Talk about your horrendous and fortuitous simultaneous luck.

❧☙

1998   Former pro wrestler Jesse Ventura was elected governor of Minnesota. To this very day, I still can't tell if that announcement was real, or if I'd just imagined it.

1955   Baseball Hall of Famer Cy Young died at age 88, after completely managing to defy his own surname.

❧☙

1880   The first cash register was patented. Unfortunately, as they'd already chosen theirs, it was too late for either the Democrats or Republicans to adopt as it a symbol.

1969   Montreal police and firemen signed a new contract with the city of Montreal, which was good, as it would've created a public relations disaster had they signed with Toronto instead.

❧☙

2007   The Writers Guild of America went on stri—

1968   Surgeons in Toronto, Canada performed the first plastic cornea implant in a human eye. The hard part was trying to coax the mannequin into signing the organ donor card.

৪০০৪

1934   The Philadelphia Eagles beat the Cincinnati Reds 64–0. In fairness however, the Reds were much more proficient that game in turning the double play.

৪০০৪

1969   Ottawa began a $50 million program to promote language training across Canada, after extensive research revealed that, evidently, very few residents could speak Canadian.

1637   Anne Hutchinson was banished as a heretic from the Massachusetts Bay Colony. Recently unearthed journals indicate the true reason was that she'd had the audacity to publicly express an opinion that was at odds with that of the mainstream media.

৪০০৪

1962   Richard Nixon announced to the media that "They won't have Nixon to kick around anymore." I can only conclude that he had meant for the rest of that particular day.

1970   New Orleans Saint Tom Dempsey set an NFL record by kicking a 63-yard field goal. Obviously, Dempsey had put his best foot forward. (*Author's Note: Whatever. It was funny enough.*)

৪০০৪

1976 A U.S.–Canadian syndicate paid $235,000 for "Hanover Hill Barb," the highest price ever paid to date for a cow. At an almost quarter million, I hope that Barb was able to at least produce chocolate milk.

1983 Amsterdam brewer Freddie Heineken was kidnapped, as evidently someone took their *Grab a Heiny* slogan just a little bit too seriously.

დრ

1970 Former French president Charles De Gaulle passed away, after ingeniously figuring out a quicker way to get an airport named after him.

1969 Sesame Street debuted on PBS. It soon became a smash hit, and quickly followed up with the spin-offs Sesame Street: Miami, Sesame Street: New York, and Sesame Street: Special Victims Unit.

დრ

1975 The ore-hauling ship Edmund Fitzgerald sank in Lake Superior. As the vessel foundered, the captain radioed to shore that he was only trying to do what he could to help get Gordon Lightfoot another hit song.

1930 A patent was awarded to Albert Einstein and Leó Szilárd for their invention, the "Einstein Refrigerator." It was marketed under the tag line, *the smarter way to chill your food.*

დრ

1493 Christopher Columbus discovered the Dutch island Saba. Typical of himself, he thought he'd landed elsewhere, and as such dubbed the natives he encountered, *Canadians.*

☞ *Also on this date: Armistice Day/Veteran's Day. To any and all veterans of the United States Armed Forces reading this—as well as all of those who aren't—you have my most sincere and enduring gratitude for your selfless service to our country. Thank you.* 🖝

1793 Jean Sylvain Bailley, the first mayor of Paris, was guillotined. Evidently, it was much worse to have low approval ratings in 18th century France than it is today.

୨୦୧୫

1910 The first movie stunt occurred, as a stunt man jumped into Hudson River from a burning balloon. The stunt man then realized it was the Hudson River he was submerged in, and fervently tried to get back into the balloon.

1987 The BBC aired its first condom commercial. Afterward, one producer described the effort to get the landmark spot on TV as "a long, hard journey."

୨୦୧୫

1942 The minimum draft age was lowered from 21 to 18, while eventually the drinking age was raised from 18 to 21. At the time, a group of young people complained, "Listen up, Congress—you are wicked lucky that, collectively, we can't be bothered with voting."

1968 The first European lung transplant took place. Afterward, the patient remarked unhappily that the doctors took him a little too literally when he'd asked them to let him get a little fresh air.

જી(જ

1851 Herman Melville's classic novel *Moby Dick* was published. One reviewer at the time called it, "simply no less than one whale of a book."

1937 The first Congressional session in air-conditioned chambers took place. It resulted in the world's first indoor rainstorm, as the cold air combined harshly when introduced to all of the hot air already being produced inside.

જી(જ

1777 The Continental Congress approved the Articles of Confederation. Though after much prodding, Congress finally admitted that they actually just read them for the pictures.

1380 French King Charles VI declared "no taxes forever." To their dismay however, the French eventually discovered that not even kings live forever.

જી(જ

1907 Oklahoma was admitted into the Union as the 46th state. I don't know; I guess I just would've expected them to be let in … Sooner.

1863   Abraham Lincoln began the first draft of his Gettysburg Address. It took him three more drafts though before he was able to accurately calculate how many score there were in 87 years.

☙❧

1928   The Boston Garden officially opened, complete with state of the art garage doors and poles to block the view of patrons who preferred to watch their ice hockey around either side of a large obstruction.

1307   William Tell shot an apple off of his son's head with a crossbow. If only YouTube had been around in 1307.

☙❧

1902   A New York toymaker named the teddy bear after Teddy Roosevelt. I guess we should just consider ourselves lucky that Grover Cleveland wasn't president in 1902.

☙❧

2004   In Little Rock, Arkansas, Bill Clinton's presidential library opened to the public. Overall, visitors found the library adequate, although with a spectacular back room.

1965   Kellogg's created their iconic Pop Tarts pastries and thus, proof of a just and loving deity was finally presented to the world.

☙❧

1985   U.S. president Ronald Reagan and Soviet leader Mikhail Gorbachev met for the first time. The meeting was called so that Gorbachev could show Reagan the benefits of eating his pizza "crust first."

⛧⛢

1998   Vincent van Gogh's *Portrait of the Artist Without a Beard* sold at auction for $71.5 million. His follow up painting, *Portrait of the Artist Without an Ear,* did not fetch nearly as much, however.

1942   The NHL abolished regular season overtime until the conclusion of World War II, as Allied commanders determined that the one thing war torn North America did not need at that time was an extra five minutes tacked on to tied hockey games.

⛧⛢

2001   Federal health officials approved the sale of the world's first contraceptive patch. While it didn't end up preventing any pregnancies, 50 percent of those who bought it eventually did stop smoking.

⛧⛢

1888   William Bundy patented the timecard clock. In a related story, millions of Americans removed William Bundy from their 1888 Christmas card lists.

1980   It was revealed on the popular TV show *Dallas* that Kristen shot J.R. Ewing, totally scrubbing my guess that it had been Barbara Eden.

৪০৪

2000   The Florida Supreme Court granted Al Gore's request to keep the presidential election recount going, evidently after he convinced them that thousands of his votes disintegrated due to rampant global warming.

৪০৪

1806   Emperor Napoleon I banned all trade with England. As a result, David Beckham stayed where he was.

1922   Howard Carter opened the tomb of King Tut. The mummy then apologized for not greeting them at the door, explaining that he'd been all wrapped up in something.

৪০৪

1992   It was reported that Senator Bob Packwood sexually harassed ten women, a revelation that ultimately caused him to resign. At his press conference, Packwood expressed regret that his unanticipated resignation would cause him to fall short of the all-time Senate record, set by Ted Kennedy.

1897   The pencil sharpener was patented and finally at long last, pencil users everywhere were able to get right to the point.

৪০৪

1955   The Cocos Islands were transferred from the United Kingdom to Australia along with seven tons of marshmallows, which Australia insisted was made part of the deal.

1969 Apollo 12 returned to Earth after the second manned mission to the moon. The return trip concluded without incident, virtually guaranteeing Apollo 12 would never get its own movie.

ಬಿCಜ

1932 The FBI Scientific Crime Detection Laboratory officially opened in Washington. It's better known today as the FBI Crime Lab, though the original employees were disappointed that J. Edgar Hoover wouldn't let them call it CSI D.C.

ಬಿCಜ

1874 Barbed wire was patented, allowing uncoordinated trespassers to get right to the point. (*Author's Note: I do wish this event occurred on November 23rd so I could've put it right under the pencil joke. And once again it is proven—timing is everything.*)

1817 The first sword swallower performed in the United States, then amazed the stunned crowd by executing his own appendectomy. No, I'm just kidding. Admit it though; that would've been pretty damn cool if he had.

ಬಿCಜ

1867 Alfred Nobel patented dynamite. After watching the destruction his new creation caused, he was inspired to fund the world's most sought after peace prize, eventually stating that TNT and peace prizes should ultimately become as companionable as peanut butter and jelly.

1961   The Pro Baseball Rules Committee voted 8–1 against legalizing the spitball. The dissenting vote came from Pitcher Gaylord Perry, who decided that that was enough to keep using it anyway.

ଚଠ

1985   Random House paid $3 million for the memoir of Richard Nixon. They didn't quite get their money's worth however, as there was an unexplained 18½ page gap in the manuscript.

1890   The first signal box for contacting the San Francisco Police Department became operational. It had to be taken down and rewired though, as whenever a citizen pulled the switch an eerie silhouette of a large bat appeared in the night sky.

ଚଠ

1839   The American Statistical Association was founded in Boston, Massachusetts. The odds against it were 318–1.

1997   The last episode of *Beavis and Butt-head,* aired on MTV. The world collectively reflected on what all of humanity had lost, and then sorrowfully went on with their lives.

ଚଠ

1995   Bill Clinton signed a bill ending the federal 55 mph speed limit, at long last allowing the four people in the United States who followed it to crank it up to 65.

1775   Sir James Jay invented invisible ink. Ok, I'll ask—how did he know?

ॐ

1972   Atari cofounder Nolan Bushnell released Pong at a tavern in Sunnyvale, California. After a few games, some players couldn't decide whether they liked it, with one telling a reporter, "I'm just not sure; I keep going back and forth with it."

1783   The United States and Britain signed the Treaty of Paris, which officially ended the Revolutionary War. The proceedings almost took an ugly turn however, when one American delegate spiked his quill pen on the table and stated loudly, "How you like us now, Bitch?"

ॐ

1993   Bill Clinton signed the Brady bill into law. It required a five-day waiting period for handgun purchases, along with background checks for buyers. Criminals, of course, simply went on getting theirs wherever they always did at their own convenience.

☞ *Born on this date: Mark Twain (1835)—Renowned American author/humorist/political satirist. Mr. Clemens was a Hartford resident who pretty much did exactly what I do. As a matter of fact, the only tangible difference between us is that Hal Holbrook never played me on stage.* ☜

DECEMBER

1918 Transylvania united with Romania, finally allowing Romanian vampires to travel back to the motherland without the annoying need for passports.

୫୦୦ଓ

1913 The first moving assembly line was introduced by the Ford Motor Company. If Hank could get all those cars to move so quick and efficiently down the line in his plant, how come he could never get them to do the same thing in traffic?

1867 Prominent English author Charles Dickens gave his first ever public reading in the United States. When asked for his opinion afterward, one audience member stated, "It was the best of readings; it was the worst of readings."

୫୦୦ଓ

1927 After almost two decades of Model T production, the Ford Motor Company unveiled the Ford Model A. Evidently after the marketing neglected to check the alphabet chart.

1775 The Grand Union Flag was flown for the first time on the USS Alfred, after being hoisted up by John Paul Jones. Jones, as was his wont, purportedly shouted out, *I have not yet begun to hoist flags!*

୫୦୦ଓ

1818   Illinois became America's 21st state. The rest of the world absorbed the news and then went on with its day, happy in the knowledge that they were all one step closer to the availability of authentic Chicago deep dish pizza.

1969   Surfer Greg Noll rode a 65 foot wave off the north shore of Oahu, the highest ocean surfing ever recorded. The only question was how he had maintained his balance while forcing the measuring tape to the ocean floor.

&0C3

1957   The Montreal Canadiens and the Toronto Maple Leafs played to a 0–0 tie, as it appears no one taught either team that in both life and in sports, it is a good thing to have goals.

1862   In Mississippi, the Battle of Coffeeville took place. Afterward the combatants, realizing they weren't quite done, moved one town over and continued the battle in Nondairycreamerville.

&0C3

633   The Fourth Council of Toledo was held, sponsored by actor Jaime Farr.

&0C3

1933   Utah ratified the 21st Amendment, which ended Prohibition and made drinking in the U.S. legal once again. Wow. Utah. Of all states to push that one over the top.

1964   The Christmas classic *Rudolph The Red-Nosed Reindeer* aired on television for the first time, exclusively on NBC. It really lit up the competition, as they didn't let more networks join in any ratings games.

જીભ્ય

1768   The Encyclopedia Britannica's first edition was published. Its only drawback was that the information contained within only went up to 1768.

1968   Richard Dodd returned a library book that had been taken out by his great-grandfather in 1923. Dodd quickly found out that while crime may not pay, honesty sure as hell does.

જીભ્ય

1926   Ontario, Canada decided against implementing Prohibition. This might be the best example ever of what is known as a "foregone conclusion."

☞   *Also on this date: Remembering Pearl Harbor (1941)—The "date that will live in infamy."* ☜

1863   Abraham Lincoln announced his plan for the Reconstruction of the South. Fortunately, not much had to be done with Mississippi.

જીભ્ય

1880   The first edition of Alberta's first newspaper, The Edmonton Bullet, was published. So ... I guess that means they were # 1—with a bullet.

1851 The first YMCA in North America was established in Montreal, Quebec. They spent a month trying to book The Village People for the opening until a media relations guy remembered that none of them would be born for another hundred years.

⛭

1974 Johnson Grigsby was freed after spending 66 years in jail. On his way out the door, he stopped to sarcastically ask the parole board if they were absolutely sure that they didn't want to wait just a little longer.

1817 Mississippi was admitted to the Union as the 20th state. To maintain the curve however, we had to give up Connecticut.

⛭

1904 Earl Grey was sworn in as Governor General at Rideau Hall in Montreal, Quebec. Forever after, the tea served there was second to none.

1620 The Mayflower landed at Plymouth Rock. After suffering irreparable damage from the rock to the ship's hull, the Pilgrims were stranded in Massachusetts for decades as their token professor tried vainly to fashion a two-way radio out of a coconut.

⛭

1844 Nitrous oxide was used for the first time in a dental procedure in Hartford, Connecticut. Though for the patient, the event turned out to be no laughing matter.

1965   Chicago Bear running back Gale Sayers scored six touchdowns, though they all went relatively for naught, as fantasy football had yet to be invented.

ഗ്രര

1787   Pennsylvania became the second state to ratify the U.S. Constitution, though as Delaware had beaten them to the punch, they were able to snag the much cooler license plate motto.

1936   The NFL championship was won by the Green Bay Packers, though it was made possible only after a last second decision by Brett Favre to play the 1936 season.

ഗ്രര

1995   In Montreal, Quebec, the new Montreal Forum was named the Molson Centre. Coincidentally, this is also what my first refrigerator was called, too.

1911   Norwegian Roald Amundsen became the first person to reach the South Pole. Upon arrival he looked around at the desolate icy wasteland, and then turned to the rest of his party as one member asked, "What the hell were we thinking?"

ഗ്രര

1999   Charles M. Schulz announced he was retiring *Peanuts*, thus throwing a blue security blanket over the most popular comic strip of all time.

1935   The Detroit Lions won the NFL championship. No, seriously.

৪০৫৪

1985   Sylvester Stallone married Brigitte Nielsen, and the real reason for Ivan Drago's rage suddenly became clear.

1997   Bill Clinton named his new Labrador retriever Buddy, after an aide wisely talked him out of his first choice, Wingman.

৪০৫৪

1971   Singer Don McLean's eight-plus minute version of *American Pie* was released. Though not exactly Payola, McLean did win the love of DJs everywhere for giving them the means to get to the restroom and back when they really needed to.

☞   *Also on this date: The Boston Tea Party. (1773) Colonists fed up with British oppression and acting on principle, protested unrepresentative taxation by throwing chests of tea into the Boston Harbor.* ☜

1895   George Brownell was granted a patent for a machine that made paper twine, proving Brownell to be clearly a man wrapped up in his work.

৪০৫৪

1903   The Wright Brothers completed the first manned flight at Kitty Hawk, North Carolina. Though the 12 second flight was deemed overall a success, Orville commented with some disappointment that the in-flight meal felt somewhat rushed.

1966   Dr. Seuss's yuletide classic *How the Grinch Stole Christmas* premiered on CBS television. It drew several complaints from viewers, though, who felt that airing the special would provide the blueprint for other potential grinches to steal future Christmases.

৪০৪৪

1865   The U.S. passed the first cattle importation law, after several incidents of people sneaking cows stashed beneath their overcoats across the Canadian border were reported.

৪০৪৪

1969   The British Parliament abolished capital punishment for murder. It kind of makes you wonder what they didn't abolish it for.

1776   Thomas Paine's famous essay *The American Crisis* was first published. It included the famous words, "these are the times that try men's souls." I'd submit that Paine should've been grateful that, unlike some of us, he wasn't a fan of Buffalo sports teams.

৪০৪৪

1843 *A Christmas Carol* by Charles Dickens was first published in England. Just missing the final cut was the forth ghost, the *Ghost of Christmas Debt to Come.*

1976 Chicago Mayor Richard Daley passed away. True to form though, he didn't allow his newly deceased status to stop him from voting in future elections.

හිඟ

1790 The first successful cotton mill in the United States began operations at Pawtucket, Rhode Island, which seems akin to the first successful L.L. Bean opening in Mobile, Alabama.

1970 Elvis Presley met with Richard Nixon in Washington, D.C., to discuss the War on Drugs, which seems akin to discussing the War on Ice Cream with Louis Anderson.

හිඟ

1913 The New York World published the first crossword puzzle. Some of the words took offence to the moniker, stating they weren't so much feeling cross but rather "mildly cantankerous."

1997 The Food and Drug Administration approved a new baldness pill for men. In a prepared statement to the press, Men's official spokesman remarked, "Thanks anyway, but we'd actually prefer a pill that *prevents* baldness."

හිඟ

1882 Thomas Edison created the first string of Christmas tree lights. Then one went out, so they all went out. His frustration in fixing them grew to the point where he scrapped the whole idea and just invented the phonograph instead.

1834 London's Joseph Hansom was issued a patent for the Hansom cab, proving you can be successful if you put the horse before the cart.

જીભ

1751 France created a plan to tax members of the clergy, an outrage that left French priests somewhat hot under the collar.

☞ *Lost on this date: My mom, Susan. (March 18, 1954–December 23, 2002) If you've read the rest of this book, you'll understand me when I say never put off any opportunity to tell a person you care about, that you do. Also, if you're not where you want to be in life, strive constantly to change that. Yes, "Life is short" is without question a tired cliché; but it's also irrefutably true.* ☜

1914 During World War I, British, French and German soldiers took it upon themselves to call a spontaneous Christmas Truce. They celebrated Christmas by playing soccer, singing carols, and trading greetings with each other. This extraordinary event showcased that sometimes subordinates can possess significantly greater intellect than their superiors.

જીભ

1997 Pope John Paul lit the first official Chanukah candle in Vatican City, temporarily suspending the unofficial Separation of Church and Church policy.

Merry Christmas

1968   NASA astronaut Frank Borman broadcast a live Christmas reading back to Earth while he was orbiting the Moon. Though I hadn't been born in 1968, I've been told that his performance that night was out of this world.

ಬಂಡ

498   The French King Clovis baptized himself on Christmas Day. I don't know much about him, but I'd say it's rather safe to assume that Clovis had himself a fairly healthy ego.

ಬಂಡ

0   Today is celebrated by Christians worldwide as the birth date of Jesus Christ in Bethlehem. Though I'm not particularly religious, whatever you believe or don't believe this "Cath-nostic" (Catholic agnostic) wishes you peace on Earth, with good will toward all.

1919   Babe Ruth was sold by the Red Sox to the Yankees. In New York, this date is also known as Thanksgiving Day.

ಬಂಡ

1973   The Exorcist opened in theatres. It turned out to be one hell of a movie.

1947   NBC first broadcast the Howdy Doody show. Though he would go on to become a television celebrity, many people contend to this very day that Doody was merely a puppet for his handlers.

ഇരേ

1871 London, England, hosted the world's first cat show. The winning feline told the press afterward that she was "indifferent" to the award. Though she then added, "but please take no offence; I'm indifferent to everything."

2008 The Detroit Lions became the first NFL team to finish the season with a perfect 0–16 record. As a result, Detroit players immediately announced a policy that for every subsequent season, they'll open a case of champagne whenever the last NFL team to get a win achieves it.

ഇരേ

1969 Mike Clark, place kicker for the Dallas Cowboys, completely missed the ball during an on-side kick attempt. This resulted in a query to his agent from the 2008 Detroit Lions regarding his availability, with Lions brass stating that they thought Clark would be a perfect fit for them.

1972 Life magazine ceased publication. Though, ironically, life still went on.

ഇരേ

1913 During the War of 1812 the British burned Buffalo, New York. Fortunately however, being Buffalo, it was quickly doused by seven feet of snow.

1993 Israel and the Vatican agreed to recognize one another. When they met, as previously agreed upon, each wore a red carnation in their respective lapel.

୫୦୯ଓ

1924   Edwin Hubble announced the existence of other galaxies. Though at a press conference later that day other galaxies stated they, however, weren't quite prepared to acknowledge the existence of Edwin Hubble.

1695   England imposed a window tax on shopkeepers, one of whom called the tax "a real pane in the ass."

୫୦୯ଓ

1862   President Abraham Lincoln signed an act admitting West Virginia to the Union. The next day he apologized to Congress, explaining that he'd had way too much to drink at the previous night's New Year's Eve Party.

AFTERWORD

In my tireless effort to save our planet, I'm recycling most of the afterword from my previous book, *Shouldn't Ice Cold Beer Be Frozen? My 365 Random Thoughts To Improve Your Life Not One Iota.* If you misinterpret this as an act of laziness, or perhaps some shameless attempt to plug my aforementioned book, realize that I'm merely taking steps to protect our Earth for the sake of future generations. That said, I hope you've enjoyed these historical quips from this unapologetic Gen-Xer. And you thought that we were all just a bunch of apathetic, self-centered, video gaming, apolitical drifters who get our news from late night TV monologues. Well, let me just tell you right here and now—I rarely play video games.

Speaking of yet another shameless plug-be sure to visit my website, www.thepassionofthechris.com, for more of my musings, writings, and voiceover work.

ABOUT THE AUTHOR

Chris Gay is a freelance writer, voice-over artist and broadcaster. He writes and broadcasts a daily, sponsored, radio humor spot in Hartford, Connecticut. He has written and voiced radio commercials, authored non-comedic freelance articles and scripts, done occasional radio color commentary for local sports, and acted a little. He lives in Connecticut, where he still awaits the return of his beloved Hartford Whalers.

Breinigsville, PA USA
01 April 2010
235329BV00003B/3/P